Reviews for
Oms From The Mat

Dana Damara reminds us in her timely new book, "Om's from the Heart" that everything that happens to us is a gift - no exceptions! Her brilliance is in taking deep-philosophical lessons from yoga and making them relatable to everyone. Her mantra of breathe, move, awaken resounds in each and every chapter and makes it not only an easy read, but a very welcome one for each of us who desire a simple journey to the soul.
-*Janet Bray Attwood, New York Times Bestseller, Co-author of The Passion Test*

Dana offers bite sized insights on how to deeply connect with one's spirit with a hipness, simplicity and potency. Her authenticity is infectious and her straight from the heart story telling riveted me until the last page. A must have!
-*Giselle Mari, Advanced Certified Jivamukti Yoga Teacher*

Dana's OMs are wonder-filled bits of awakening. As she shares her own blossoming moments, you'll find in reading them that you are opening, as well.
-*Michele McKeag Larsen, founder and chief joy officer of The Joy Team*

Dana exudes in her writing the power and presence she brings to her yoga classes. Her honest stories and practical real-life wisdom will inspire and empower readers to move beyond their limiting beliefs to create the lives they deserve.
-*Stephanie Adams, ERYT 500, Founder, Flow Yoga Studio & Jaya Yoga Teacher Training*

Dana's book is an eloquent sampling of the beauty of yoga and how to manifest it in our lives, a must read.
-*Tiffany Cruikshank, international yoga teacher, author & wellness expert at the Nike World Headquarters*

Dana's reflections on love and life as a yogi makes this book the perfect bedside companion. Written in short bursts of inspiration, this book is a series of lovely reminders of not only who we want to be but who we already are. A refreshing breeze of positivity. Well done!
-*Kathryn Budig, international yoga teacher, yogi-foodie*

This book is more than a book to me, it is a spiritual tool of healing wisdom for the soul, your words get me through my day.
- *Stephanie Van Alen, Artist, VAN ALEN CUSTOMS*

Make yourself a cup of tea and carve out some space to surrender to the wisdom that flows from this book of OMS. What you will discover is you have the power to breathe life into your energy body, and the spiritual stamina to finally meet your true Self on the mat.
-*Edie Summers, Author of The Memory of Health, Certified Wellness Coach*

Foreword
by Cori Martinez, Asha Yoga

Once when my daughter was three months old, she was screaming in my arms. She had been crying for hours- for months actually. She cried a lot the entire first year of her life. This particular moment I had the thought that I couldn't take it anymore, that she had to stop crying or I was going to go crazy. I felt a surge of anger, and then panic, and then I realized… there appeared to be nothing I could do to stop her from crying. So maybe my job was not to fix everything and make it better, but just to be there for her in her pain. I took a deep breath and continued to rock her. I felt the comfort of acceptance, of not resisting, and I held her for over an hour more while she continued to cry.

Through my years of practicing and teaching yoga I have come to believe that the universe is friendly. -That it gives us only exactly what we need for our own human and spiritual evolution. I never even knew to ask for the ability to be with my daughter through her pain without needing to fix it if I couldn't. And yet I was given that gift, and have become a better mother because of it. There have been many times since that day when I have tried again, unsuccessfully, to "fix it"… and the moment I know it's not possible I can be intimate with her in a way I cannot be as the problem solver.

We all have the opportunity to learn from every experience, to trust in life and lean in to the gift of each moment… but we have to pay attention. Dana Damara is a woman who pays attention. In this book she eloquently explores moments of her life that could belong to any of us; moments that could be ordinary and often missed if she wasn't so open, so close, so tuned in to the opportunity that is always there. Because she looks so closely and is willing to share with us what she sees, readers of her confessions have the opportunity to be opened as well.

As I read this book I am inspired to lean in to the moments of my own life, even a little closer, and see the sweetness that I may otherwise have missed.

This opportunity is now yours… enjoy!
– Cori Martinez, Asha Yoga

Breathe, Move, Awaken
to the Power of Yoga

Acknowledgments

This book, *Oms from the Mat,* is a compilation of spiritual inspirations born from a love of movement on the yoga mat. When we stay stagnant in our bodies, we remain stagnant in our minds and our hearts. Yoga is the catalyst that shifts and opens the body…allowing our physical body to harmonize with our spirit and our mind.

Each chapter of this book offers easy to read devotionals that will resonate with where you are right now and allow you to journey to the center of your Self. Easy to read and playful, enjoy these Oms in succession or randomly.

This book would not have made it to print without the help of so many individuals. I am in deep gratitude and can feel the energy of the Earth around my heart as I write this. Thank you Diana Howes for seeing the gift or writing within me before I saw it within myself. Your vision and spark is what gave me the wings to begin my flight. Thank you to my ex-husband, Tony Layon, for always being there along my path of growth and transformation. Our road was not an easy one but you always stood tall and stoic. These Oms couldn't have been written without your help; our babies were so small and needed so much. You were and always will be, a powerful support for me and our girls. I am so blessed to have you along my path.

Thank you to Kent Gustavson with Blooming Twig Books for seeing this vision and making the first go around a reality for me. You brought manifestation to my dream. Thank you to Kathy Carlisle and Traci Weisshar for taking that most amazing road trip with me to Tahoe. That was a door that flew open and without your companionship, authenticity and love I may have never walked through it. You were there for me during a very challenging time and provided the stability I needed to really learn how to stand alone.

Thank you to one of my greatest teachers, Seane Corn and the entire team of Off the Mat, Into the World for pushing me to even higher heights of my own truth. Your vision for the world has sparked clarity around my personal vision as well as my personal power.

Thank you to Lance Jordan, my dearest, oldest friend from many lifetimes ago. Our paths are crossed for eternity. Thank you for taking the time to love me and my daughters and thank you for taking us to the place that brought the cover photo to life.

Thank you to Angie Cherry and Michele Larsen, two of my most favorite people in the world for believing in this project. For donating your time and talent to me, to our community and to the betterment of humankind. You are an inspiration and a gift that I feel blessed to be able to play with in this lifetime.

Thank you to God for always being near me, within me and guiding me through my journey. That higher power we seek is within us every moment of every day if we listen. Thank you to my parents for letting me go time and time again, giving me the freedom I needed to finally see my own truth and my own strength.

And to all the angels who have touched my path so far in this lifetime, I am in deep gratitude and grace knowing that you share your gift with this world and I am a beneficiary. We are all here for each other, we are all One and with that knowledge I am at peace and can finally share these words and inspirations.

With enormous amounts of gratitude I offer you *Oms from the Mat; Breathe, Move, Awaken to the Power of Yoga*. Thank you for taking this journey. You are a gift to this world and it's time to shine!

Much love and grace,
Dana Damara

To Isabella and Ava, my daughters

The day you were born I was touched by the hand of God. In every moment you allow me to see myself as a Divine gift to the Universe. You are joy, love, source...you *are* God. My heart overflows with love every minute of my day knowing that you picked me to be your mother. You may not always understand the decisions I make; you may not always understand the logical world that you live in; you may not always like how things show up in your life. But remember this: You are always being guided by the hand of God. You are always backed up by the Universe. You are a co-creator with God Himself.

You know this...YOU reminded me. Keep that knowledge always...keep that belief in your heart no matter what shows up in your life. You hold this Universal truth, share that belief, my dear angels.

Table of Contents

Chapter 1

On Fear Versus Security
Root Chakra: Muladhara

Distractions

Do you ever feel distracted by all that happens in one day? Distracted by all the e-mail, voice mail, and task lists that seem to be a daily obligation? Do you tend to look at life as overwhelming and daunting? When we feel overwhelmed, we miss out on the opportunities coming toward us because we can't focus long enough in that moment before moving on to the next task. Our focus is distracted and out of alignment with all the clutter around us.

Did you know that we receive more information in one day than people 100 years ago received in an entire lifetime?

That statistic really opened my eyes and made me stop and gasp. Is all this information really that important? We allow these distractions to dictate our day and consequently our days get away from us. Before we know it, our day is over and nothing happened the way we intended.

Something has to give when we are in that state of doing instead of being. We aren't in alignment with our true Self because we feel overwhelmed. The key is to ask yourself, "How important is the information that I am receiving right now? Is it integral to the intention I have set for the day?"

If it's not… let it go. Create a task list and break it down into sections. One section can be labeled FOR TODAY. Another can list tasks FOR THE WEEK. And another can be called SOON. Color code them if you are a visual learner. See what works for you.

What you may find out is that you have more time when you prioritize. Not only that, but the items listed under SOON may even take care of themselves simply because you stated them as an intention but left the completion up to the Universe. You released tension around the task and allowed the Universe to line it up for you.

Give your burdens to the Universe and all will be taken care of. The time you need will manifest itself and you will see that you have more time than you can imagine.

Leap of Faith

When faced with a decision that could be life-changing, what is the natural response? Most often it's fear, doubt, or worry. Why make the change when you can continue on the road that feels easy? Fear, doubt, and worry are limiting emotions that keep you in a state of just maintaining. It's in those moments of change that you are challenged to learn, evolve, and transform if you are prepared to let go of those limiting beliefs that are rooted in fear.

It has been explained to me in the following way... Transformation is like being a flying trapeze artist. It's that moment when you know you have to let go of the ring that has sustained you in order to get to the next ring. That moment of letting go is fearful for most of us. The "what ifs" begin creeping into our consciousness and we may stay complacent in our comfortable world.

But what are we missing out on by not taking that leap of faith? Who could we become? What could transform for us? It's in those moments that we are given the opportunity to leap, to become and to see our true, authentic Self. This is life; it's why we are here! The best part about transforming ourselves is that we give others the permission to find transformation within themselves as well. It's amazing for this world!

I challenge you to think about a time or situation when you were fearful of change. What did you do? I challenge you to ask yourself to be present, to notice when it is being offered, and then to leap toward it—letting go of fear, worry, and doubt.

It will change your life.

Stillness

Have you read *A New Earth* by Eckhart Tolle? It's phenomenal. But so is *Growing the Positive Mind* by Dr. William Larkin. And even more amazing is *Ask and It Is Given* by Jerry and Esther Hicks. Just recently I watched two fabulous movies: *Heart Math* with Gregg Braden and *The Moses Code*. These were truly inspiring, eye-opening movies. I am amazed at what is out there for all of us to learn from: amazed at how conscious our society is becoming.

It's exciting to think that enough of us are asking for transformation and change is finally happening! But there is something else to consider here; conscious activities and situations come to you when you are ready. They have always been out there, waiting… waiting for you to notice and say yes.

These books and movies didn't fall into my lap by coincidence. I attracted them to me because I was asking for information like this, and there are a lot of you out there doing the same thing.

For a time; each and every book I picked up talked about using meditation to quiet the mind—to find our center, our inner peace, our joy, our purpose. Why is that?

Because at the time I was searching for peace. We all want joy. We want to understand why we are here. And how do we find that? Through stillness and meditation. Through honest awareness of our inner voices. Our society as we know it now, is collectively waking up!

All those books and movies are feeding us the same message: SLOW DOWN! They are telling us that we have become a society that moves so quickly that we have forgotten how to stop. We have forgotten that it's OK to sit and be still, to say, "I deserve to take this time out for me." The illusion is that there is always something to do, somewhere to be, or something more important than just being.

If you want to truly find joy, balance, and purpose, just sit and breathe. Not too difficult if you can find the time, right? My suggestion is to make the time…today. Look at all the things on your "to do" list right now. Ask yourself, "Where am I on this list?"

You don't need to "meditate"; you can pick up a good book, listen to some great music that makes you sing, walk your dog, play with your kids. You can sit and watch the wind. Do anything that brings you joy and be in that moment and that moment only. Be one with it and know that this is where you are supposed to be right now and nowhere else.

Stillness provides clarity which brings about joy. Try it.

Separate from Our Ego

When I look back into the past, I can't help but realize how many opportunities we are offered to grow, transform, and evolve. One of my favorite sayings is, "When we set out to transform others and if we are open, we can't help but transform ourselves."

This resonates with me so very much because I know that even though I am a yoga "teacher," I am really nothing more than a yoga student sharing information I believe to be true. This fact and realization humbles me each time I step on my mat. Each one of us has a gift to offer our community; a gift to share with the world and we are meant to express it endlessly. I have always said this in class but it is a truth that now, after personal life experiences, really resonates deep within my heart.

As I continued to read Eckhart Tolle's book, *A New Earth*, I was amazed at how eloquently he wrote about how we are all so very separate from our egos, how as we move toward this higher consciousness of living, we become the spiritual beings we were meant to be. And, as a growing number of us become more aware and "awakened," the quicker our consciousness evolves. Most importantly, I understood how we will begin to truly see WHO we are sooner if we can dis-identify ourselves with our ego.

After reading the *Yoga Sutras* (for the fifth time), I am reminded that this process of moving toward a higher state of consciousness IS yoga. The postures were actually created physiologically to do this. This is what yoga instructors have been relaying in their classes for years. And maybe some instructors knew this when they decided to teach yoga. Maybe they understood the

magnitude of what they were doing all along. But honestly, I didn't truly understand this powerful truth right away; but when I embraced it, it changed my life both dramatically and swiftly.

I understood the true power of yoga in all its glory when an Om got stuck in my throat and I was on the verge of tears, not comprehending why. That reaction was my body responding to something that needed to be expressed so it could be "rewired."

We all have our own journey. It just so happened that mine started with using yoga specifically as a physical practice for my body. It could have stayed that way forever and I would have been fine with that had I not explored the deeper dimensions of yoga. However, all this other stuff just makes this journey that much sweeter.

Whatever your intention as you head to your first yoga class, know that it is exactly where you need to be in that moment. Meet yourself where you are. You will find the class that fits your intention and it will find you. Have no expectations and lose all judgment about everything: the instructor, , the facility you choose, the students, how your perform. Lose it all and be open.

I am deeply honored and grateful to be sharing yoga with others. And I am humbled by your courage and strength to make a difference in yourself and in those around you.

Time

As my kids grow, I am more and more delighted at what conscious beings they are. How grateful I am to witness these little spirits living life. They teach me so very much.

It could be the way they intently pour water from one cup into the other just to see what happens. It also could be the way they run around the backyard laughing loudly at nothing at all. Mostly I notice how conscious they are when I'm ushering them into the car in the morning for school. One of them will inevitably say, "Mom, look at this flower!" I am stopped in my tracks to

look at something so small and beautiful, something I would have never noticed in my hastiness to arrive in the next moment.

They are completely immersed in the present moment all the time; they know nothing else! This phenomenon made me wonder what it was they have that we, as adults, have lost?

And I quickly realized that it's the negation of time. They truly have no concept of time.

The other day it hit me like a ton of bricks when I said to my five-year-old daughter, "Sit on your bed for five minutes while you think about what you did." She responded by saying, "Mommy, I don't know how long five minutes is!" She was frustrated, but I realized how fortunate she was not be ruled by time.

It's time that takes us away from the present moment. It's time that brings about stress, anxiety, and worry. It's time that defines what comes "next." We lose the beauty of the present moment when we are ruled by time.

As human beings we need time for practical purposes, of course. We have appointments and commitments. It's inevitable. But what we tend to do is already be in that future moment while we are getting there. We worry about being on time, worry we will forget something, worry we won't get our usual spot in yoga class. We are so focused on time that we miss the beauty in the moment of now.

I challenge you today to notice life around you. Remember to start your day off with breath. Set your intention to be present. When people are talking to you, really listen. Listen without waiting for them to finish so you can say something. When you're getting into the car in the morning for work, take a second to stop and look around you. Notice something magnificent.

One morning after writing this, my girls and I whistled to the birds and waited to hear them sing back to us for an entire week. They made me do it every day and I am so grateful for that experience. When your kids are in present moment, just watch them. If you don't have kids, notice the ones in the park, in the store, or anywhere around you; notice how present they are. They are amazing creatures and they have a lot to teach us "grown-ups."

Be Yourself

Every week I sit down to write an Om and I search for inspiration. As a single mother of two young girls, woman entrepreneur and friend of many amazing individuals, I don't need to look very far. That doesn't mean life is perfect. It just means that on a consistent, daily basis, I am offered opportunities to grow, transform, and to live to my highest potential.

The opportunities don't always come in nicely decorated gift boxes labeled *peace, joy, and tranquility* either. Actually, just the opposite is true. Transformation mostly happens in difficult situations, unruly children, and with the constant burning question, "Am I doing this right?"

Just the other day, my daughter came home crying, saying:

"Mom, so-and-so wouldn't let me play with her unless I knew the password. And I didn't know it so I didn't have anyone to play with. It made me sad because I really like her. Why doesn't she like me?" As I searched for how to answer that question, I immediately remembered my childhood. My eyes welled up with tears as I remembered girls being "mean" to me in school, too. I wanted to take all the hurt away from my daughter and I knew this was an opportunity to teach her something.

I don't remember what my mom told me during times like these, but I am sure it was loving and supportive with the undertone of, "So what? Who cares about them?" and, maybe, "Wait until I see that girl's mom at the next PTA meeting… " As a child, I do remember, however, being very sad and hurt and wondering what I should do differently so that these girls would like me.

In the five seconds I had before I answered my daughter, I remembered that we are all connected. I also remembered that it's not possible for everyone to like us. In fact, if everyone liked us, the Universe would be completely out of balance. If everyone liked us, we couldn't possibly be living up to our most authentic Self because how could we possibly be all things to all people? I am sure this is somewhat close to what my mom tried to tell me and sort of what I tried to tell my daughter.

So if we are all connected, and it doesn't matter if everyone likes us our not, why are we not our most authentic selves? Why aren't we just "doing our thing" and finding this daily bliss and joy that yogis talk about? Why are we still worrying about what people will think? Why are we living with limits, rules, and boundaries about who we "should" be?

It's because somewhere along the line, someone told us that we had limits. Someone told us to be serious. Someone told us to be nice and they told us how to behave so people would like us. Someone told us to face reality. What IS reality anyway? Isn't our perception of the present moment the ONLY reality we have?

The only moment in time that holds any power is the present moment.

Obviously there are standards of conduct that we, as a society, need to follow. But are there boundaries to being who you truly are, your most authentic Self? No, there are not. We can all be who we are meant to be and enjoy being in that space. If you don't know who you are at your most raw place, take some time out to breathe, meditate, walk silently, ask yourself questions, wait for answers, and get there. It's a great place to be.

In the end, I said to my daughter, "It's OK that so-and-so doesn't like you. Not everyone can like you every single day. Maybe tomorrow will be different. What game do you like to play? Who else can play with you? What other friends would you like to get to know? Do you want to show me the game you would like to play?" If I teach her anything, I want her to know that all that matters is that she feels good about herself, no matter what other people think.

Be yourself. Play your own game. Beat your own drum. Sing loud and strong! You are you and you are beautiful. It's OK if everyone doesn't like you; your spirit will be happy and that will radiate out into the world.

Remember, we are all connected. Be kind to others, for in that moment we are showing kindness to ourselves.

Believe

Yesterday, I received a stone from a friend of mine that she found near the Great Pyramids in Egypt. I was astonished at the story she told me about the stone. She told me that the stone was blessed and that it had power in it. She told me that after meditating with this stone for some time, it began to jump in her hands.

Stories like this renew my spirit; they fill me with peace and faith after a harsh day of "reality." They remind me that we have the power within us to manifest that which we desire if we believe, if we are in love with the idea of creating the life we are destined to live.

I am considered by some to be a bit "woo-woo" because I completely believe in this type of stuff. I have also been told that I am Pollyannaish and look at life with rose-colored glasses. Many times people have asked me throughout my lifetime of choices, "What if this happens and what if that happens?" or "What the heck are you thinking?"

The ironic thing is, I have always done what I have set out to do. Sometimes the decisions haven't seemed to be the best, but the experience and the journey led me to something better so I know there was always a reason for each choice I made.

The most important lesson here is: if you believe, you can achieve. If you believe you can parachute out of a plane, you can! If you believe you can start your own business, you can! If you believe those stones are jumping in your hands, they are! We create the pictures of our lives; the daily distractions test our beliefs. Stay true to that which you believe in and your life will unfold as it should. Listen to your heart and it will always speak your truth.

Victimization

Ever have something happen in your life and you hear yourself say, "Why is this happening to me?" We have all done it. Whatever it is—a broken relationship, stopped traffic, a bad day—we have all played the victim in situations like these. How about if the next time you hear yourself say those words, you turn it around and say, "Why is this happening FOR me?"

As we all know, experiences are gifts; they may not look like it sometimes, but they are. They are gifts from the Universe allowing us space to recognize what it is within ourselves that can evolve.

They are gifts of time for us to witness the light within us. Everything that happens in our lives is a gift and we are offered this opportunity for growth toward our most authentic Self. Most often, we are so comfortable with where we are, surrounded by the friends, the job, and the "things" that define us, that we may choose to ignore that voice of knowing. We may choose to stay where we are and not evolve to our higher Self. But those opportunities will keep coming until we realize the gifts they offer and we act upon them in an open, compassionate, honest way.

Changing your perception, from victim mentality to someone who expresses gratitude for everything, will change your life immediately. Notice the gifts around you and breathe next time you hear yourself say, "Why does this always happen to me?" Rephrase it: "Why is this continually happening for me? What am I to be learning? Where is the gift?" It's there; be open to receive it.

Blissfully Ignorant

I had the opportunity to watch a video of myself at my wedding several years back. As a human being and not an "enlightened yogini," my egotistical mind went directly to "Oh my gosh! Look how skinny and tan I was!" For a while I couldn't get past how young, vibrant, and happy I looked. For a few minutes, my ego was saying, "What happened? You looked so happy then."

And then a little voice said, "Wisdom, enlightenment, empowerment, peace. You are on the crest of a wave to your higher Self." And I thought, yes, that's it.

I sat up and looked a little closer at myself on the video. Although I looked happy, I also wondered if I was I truly happy, or was I ignorantly blissful? I believe yes, I was very happy, but did I know my Self? I had an idea of who I was but, no, I did not know my Self then. I did not yet understand how to tap into my Higher Power.

But we are where we are when we are because that is where we choose to be. And we can't know what we know until we know it. Sounds like a cliché and like I'm talking in circles, but it is the truth. You've heard people say, "I wish I knew then what I know now." We did know it then; we just didn't remember it.

We are put here to remember who we are at our deepest soul level. We start off as this blissful spirit. Then life lessons hit us hard. From the time we are babies to the time we die, we experience life lessons. The lessons aren't here to "teach" us anything per se; they are here for us to remember what our Higher Purpose is as we grow, experience life, and become the Beings we were meant to be.

Neal Donald Walshe said it so eloquently in *Conversations with God* when he wrote:

> "You have denied for so long Who You Are that you have forgotten Who You Are."

This means to me that we know who we are but life happens and we forget. We let what others think, do, and say to us create a false reality of who we are. But we know, at our deepest level of being, who we are; we just know. Another quote from the same book says:

> "You are, therefore, in the process of experiencing yourself by creating yourself anew in every single moment."

Wow! So that means we have this life opportunity to become our highest Self! What a gift! And this is not to say that we need to "fix" ourselves. We are perfect, exactly where we are. We can spend months in therapy trying to figure out what went wrong or we can surrender to what is right now. We are just given opportunities to fine-tune our Self if we choose to take them.

Notice opportunities in your life as they arise and ask yourself, "If I were to know the highest image of myself, what would that look like?" Then ask, "How will these experiences that I am having right now bring me closer to that image of myself?"

It's empowering to know that we are given this gift of life to recreate ourselves anew when we choose. Choose happiness and joy every time.

Open to Grace

Yoga advertisements really inspire me. One in particular I still remember was a picture of a yogi, arms held high, heart space open, with the caption, "Open to grace."

The first time I read that I thought, "I'm going to use that affirmation in my class!" I did and it was amazing to see how everybody shifted just a bit. Their hearts opened more, their arms lifted higher, and I could feel the deep breathing of everyone in the room.

Then one day I was listening to Dr. Michael Beckwith and Mary Manin-Morrissey discuss space for grace. The question was, "What does it mean to "open to grace?" Perfect, I thought. Now at least I can understand what it is that I am sharing in class, because sometimes, I admit, ideas just come to me and I share them—not because I know all the answers, but because I know how great I feel when I am thinking, speaking, or acting out what I have learned.

What I learned is this: grace is that place where life flows. It's where we hear the wind, see the sun, see the colors of the Universe around us, and we flow naturally with nature. It's in those moments of joy when we realize that we don't have to work so hard to get what we want. We can just allow the space for grace to happen so that situations, people, and events can flow easily to us without the resistance or effort we create by trying to figure it all out.

Mary Manin-Morrissey said, "Life can get easier if we go with the flow of life which knows its own nature."

When we come to yoga class, we are freeing the mind so we can allow space for grace. That's why yoga feels so good. Everything is still. With quiet meditation and contemplation, we are free to notice what the Universe is delivering to us. When we move and breathe in and out of certain postures that open our hearts, we are physically feeling openness within us.

Next time you find yourself trying to "figure it all out," for example, what to do about finances, your relationship, your job, or what decision to make, sit still for a moment. Breathe, watch the breeze, smell the flowers, and then listen for the answers. They will come to you if you are open.

If this is too challenging for you, try this exercise instead. Take a vase or a bowl that you don't use anymore. On a small piece of paper (or several pieces), write what it is that is troubling you. What is getting in the way of you living "gracefully" or "in the flow?" Offer up your worries, your doubts, and your troubles.

For example: "I am worried about what will happen to my financial situation if I quit my job."

And then fold these pieces of paper in half so you can't read them from the outside. Put them in the vase or bowl and put the vase or bowl somewhere up high on a shelf or something. When you're done, breathe for a little while and say to yourself, "I'm giving these worries up to the Universe. I trust that all is well." Breathe that in and out for as long as you need to and then walk away, promising yourself to no longer worry about those things. Have true faith that it will work out. Symbolically, you are releasing your worries and allowing space for grace.

When you set an intention about something you want to do, be, or contribute, instead of asking how, just breathe in space and allow the Universe to deliver. It delivers, every single time.

I Am

Think about how often you use the words "I am" throughout your day. I am tired; I am broke; I am stressed out; I am overworked. Any of those sound familiar? How many times do you hear yourself saying the following? I am blissful; I am fulfilled; I am abundant; I am vibrant. I would bet that the majority of people are attaching negative endings to their "I am" statements.

When we say "I am," we are creating that which we believe to be true. If you believe you are tired, you will be tired. If you believe you are vibrant, you will be vibrant. It's like Henry Ford said, "If you think you can or you can't, either way, you are right."

We create that which we desire and believe we deserve for ourselves in this lifetime. We are creative beings and the two most powerful words in the English language are "I am." Saying "I am" is like summoning all the "powers who be" to us. They are just waiting.

Begin listening to yourself. If you can't hear yourself, begin listening to others around you when they use "I am" statements.

I am giving you a challenge. Next time you hear someone say "I'm exhausted," for example, look at the person and say something like, "Wow, you don't look like it. In fact, you look great!" Witness the transformation your words create for them.

Notice yourself using these negative words and phrases. Then stop yourself dead in your tracks and reverse it. There are no more powerful words than "I am." Use them wisely.

Peace with What Is

I have the pleasure to be the one in our household who hangs out with our girls in the morning, connects through breakfast and candid discussion, and then drops them off at school.

I am also the one who picks them up every day. As a business owner, I realize this is an incredible gift that I am grateful for each day. When I arrive at 3:15 p.m., they are so excited to see me. At that moment, I feel more love than I can even begin to describe.

Some days are smooth and everyone is happy and content. Then there are days when there are tears, sniffles, little sad voices begging, "Mommy, can we please stay home today?" They hold onto my leg shyly as I say, "Be brave. You know you will have fun today. Mommy has to go to work now." I try to get them to join other children, hoping they will cooperate and walk in with a friend, but most often it doesn't work.

I try bribing them with gum or ice cream after school. But when all cajoling fails, I hear myself saying, "Enough already. Mommy has to go now. You will be fine. We do this every day. Come on now, give mommy a break."

Those are the days I ask myself, "Am I doing the right thing? Am I missing out?" I beat myself up with self-doubt thinking, "What could be more important than raising my kids? I can't believe I am actually working." But just because I'm working, does that mean I'm not in the "game" of raising my kids? Or is it simply that my way of doing it is a little different than other people's ways?

Who made the rules about what was "right" in raising our kids anyway? And my, how those rules sure have changed over the years.

What a balancing act for us mothers these days; we actually have choices! I read a book to my kids one night that showed Barbie taking Kelly and Stacey to school and the caption read in a sing-songy kind of way, "Good luck today, Kelly. Have fun. I will see you when your day is done."

Until that moment, I didn't know that Barbie was a working mom! I don't think that was the case when I was in school. But that's the case now, isn't it? And really, it's not such a bad thing. I mean, our mothers and grandmothers may have loved the opportunity to do something out of the house if given the chance, but for the most part, they weren't offered that opportunity.

As contemporary mothers, we are so fortunate to have choices. Stay home or work. Whatever we choose, we can either beat ourselves up or be happy with our decision.

Remember that kids are so intuitive. If we are happy with our job outside the home, they will feel that. If we aren't, they will feel that, too. If we are confused about what is right, they pick up on that also.

If we can know our truth, we can stand in it and tell them how we really feel. And it's much easier to explain and discuss our choices when they serve ourselves, our family, and our higher purpose, isn't it?

What message does that send to our children? Do what you love. Find balance and joy in all that you do. Not a bad start for a 3-year-old.

If you stay home with your kids, cherish each moment. Yes, I know it's hard; I did it and I am such a better mom when I work. Remember that each of us is different. And when we become moms, our perception of life and our priorities shift. We all view the world differently. Stay open to that without judgment of others or ourselves.

Find balance and peace with your decisions. I heard myself saying a couple of months ago, "I can't possibly do all this!" And I proceeded to rattle through all the things I do during my day. I was overwhelmed, tired, and unhappy. Then one night during meditation, I heard the words, "Yes you can. You are doing it."

Make the choices that make you most happy. Go to work and love your job. When you come home, be home and be present. The biggest gift you can give your kids is undivided attention. With technology and information at our fingertips, it may be difficult to turn off your cell phone or computer while playing or reading with your kids. Do it anyway.

The key is to find balance, joy, and peace once we have made our decision to stay home or work. And most of all, be kind to yourself. Find balance and peace in all that you do. Times will never slow down; there will always be something to take care of, fold, put away and think about. Find peace amidst all that "chaos" and instead, call it the joy of living a completely fulfilled and abundant life!

Focused Attention

I came home the other day to my kids singing this made-up rendition of the "focus" song, sung to the tune of "Frère Jacques." I was amazed and intrigued all at the same time. Apparently they had been listening to me when I told them, "Focus. For just one second, breathe and focus." The song was cute and informational and ended with "Thank you, everybody" and a curtsy.

I understand the attention span of a 3-year- old is naturally pretty short. I witness my kids going from one thing to another fairly quickly on some days. It got me thinking, do we, as parents, encourage this behavior? Then I asked myself when the last time was that I showed them I was focused on one thing at a time. Don't I make dinner, talk on the phone, and help them both create some artistic masterpiece out of Q-tips all that same time?

How many times have we complimented ourselves on being able to get "so many things done at one time!" With the way technology has advanced and will continue to advance, we will be more apt to do more than one thing at a time. Why? One reason: because we can. The lure will be that we will become more efficient, more effective, and more task-oriented.

When we do this, our ability to be completely present in one moment is compromised. How are we supposed to enjoy the moment when we are scattered, trying to focus on the outcome, the phone call or e-mail coming in, the television program, the Halloween costume we are making, the cookies that are baking and, oh yeah, our child, spouse, or friend talking about their day—all at the same time?

Where are we in all this multitasking? Unconscious, that's where. We are riding this wave of "have-to's," trying to squeeze all this information in and ending up feeling more exhausted than we did when we started.

The more I contemplate simple life issues like multitasking, the more I turn to my yoga practice to find the answers. And keep in mind, yoga is not only about moving on your mat. It's much more than that. It's been around a long, long time and many of the philosophies and ideas can be related to current issues simply and eloquently.

Judith Lasater has some very great advice in her book *Living Your Yoga* about multitasking. She says:

> "Discipline is truly expressed by my intention to stay present in each moment. Whether it is driving my kids to school, standing in line at the grocery store, paying bills, interacting with coworkers, finishing a task on time, or practicing yoga, if I do it with a deep intimacy for each moment, then I am truly disciplined. Without that intimacy, I am merely performing a series of mechanical actions."

Do you ever have days when your entire day is a series of mechanical actions? I know I have days like that every single week.

For one week, I challenge you to do just one thing at a time. When someone is talking to you, stop doing what you are doing and listen. When you are driving your kids to school, turn off the radio and ask them what they are excited about doing that day. Turn off your cell phone or computer the minute you get home and interact with your family, listen to some music, or read a book. Sit in your backyard and enjoy the sounds of the grasshoppers.

Just do one thing at a time.

Slow down. Begin each new activity throughout your day with an inhale and exhale, letting go of expectation of that activity and allowing it to unfold before you. Let your mantra be, "I have more than enough time."

Acknowledging Our Accomplishments

How many times have you said the following to yourself? "I wish I had done this" or "Why didn't I do that?" or, better yet, "I wish I had known all this earlier in my life."

Let's keep it real, shall we? We can only know what we know. And we can only make decisions based on our knowledge at any given moment in our lives. Our "knowingness" can only be in direct proportion to what we choose to understand at any given point. Why, then, do we beat ourselves up for not

knowing everything, having everything, and not getting it right every single time?

It's because we continually compare ourselves to others and judge ourself based on what others are doing, what they have, and what they are contributing.

In yoga we share the importance of letting go of competition, judgment, and expectation of ourselves and of others. That seems simple enough on the mat, what about off the mat?

We are each on our own journey, our own path, our own Divine course. Along our path of life, we make thousands of choices every day that bring us to our own present moment.

Want to take inventory of your life? Take some time to sit down and write a "resume" of your life. Keep it simple but write down, in a fairly chronological order, all the great things you have done, all the things you are proud of, and include some of the exceptional choices you have made in your life.

Some examples of how simple it can really be are: graduated high school, bought my first car, went to college, took care of my (grandma, mother), moved into my own place, secured a job I love, traveled Europe, started a business, raised kids, planted a garden, painted my bedroom.

Whatever you are inspired by, write it down!

Read through it and then acknowledge those accomplishments for how fabulous they truly are. Remember what it felt like to actualize those accomplishments. And then post it somewhere you can see it all the time. These are the choices you made in your life that brought you to where you are right now. Notice all the amazing things you have done with your life and say out loud, "I ROCK!"

You *do* have a say in which direction your life goes. You *do* get to make the decisions that bring you here now. When you reflect, notice how each choice was made with passion and intention and the importance that decision held for you at that point in time.

Understand that you do have a choice and how fortunate that simple fact is for us all. Be inspired by all you do and have done. You are amazing.

Abundance

One of the greatest books I have ever read was *Living Your Yoga* by Judith Lasater. Her writing puts Patanjali's Yoga Sutras in a perspective that even I can relate to. Reading the Yoga Sutras can be a little intimidating to a yoga-virgin, so applying them to modern day scenarios really helped me when I began my spiritual journey.

In one chapter, she writes about abundance and how there is always enough for everyone. She talks about how we have been conditioned to believe there isn't enough. This has created a collective feeling of lack and greed in our society. This can be quite an easy trap to fall into if we are not aware of this conditioning.

The truth is, there is always enough for everybody. There is no reason to hold on to things simply because we think we won't get anymore. Quite the contrary— remember the saying, the more you give, the more you get?

I had the opportunity to experience this firsthand at my daughters' school playground. A little boy had made a huge leaf pile. All the little kids were so amazed with his creation they began taking leaves for themselves from his pile. It was really blissful to watch these kids, amazed by the beauty of the leaves.

The creator of the original leaf pile, however, was not happy. He was crying and yelling at the kids to stop. It was his leaf pile. He had worked so hard on it! I watched the teachers tell the other kids no, that was his leaf pile. Then I watched the other kids cry and stomp away.

What was ironic to me was, without realizing it, the other kids were stomping toward thousands of leaves strewn about on the lawn, just waiting to be noticed. There was an abundance of leaves right there in front of them, but they didn't even notice.

So why did that little boy get so upset? And why didn't those other children notice the abundance of leaves? Conditioning?

What would happen if we opened our eyes and looked at what we *do* have instead of what we do not? We may begin to notice the abundance that is true for all of us: there is more than enough for everyone.

Take a look—there is an abundance of leaves right in your own backyard.

Daily Yoga

Have you ever started a disciplined yoga practice and then life happens and you just can't seem to make it work for your schedule anymore? You have these visions of yourself making time to practice every week, maybe even three times a week, and then you miss class one week, and then another week, and all of a sudden, a month has gone by and you haven't been to one yoga class.

Let me shed some light on this situation just a bit so you don't feel badly. Yoga postures are only a small part of a true yoga practice; in fact, only 13% of yoga is about the postures. You are actually practicing yoga every day, off your mat, in every *other* aspect of your life!

How can I say this? It's easy! Take, for example, the life of a yoga teacher. Teaching yoga is simple. There's no stress involved, ever.

We shut the door, meditate, and practice asana for over an hour. There are no distractions during that time, just one hour of stillness. But couldn't we all experience that stillness and "enlightenment" given those circumstances of physically blocking out all distraction? Metaphorically shutting the door on our life?

I don't know about you, but for me, life at home is quite the opposite. In fact, my life is all about distractions! As my children grow, there is more to do, more incessant noise, more opinions, and much less silence.

At home, we are presented with the real self, the one who has "faults" and "issues" and "things to work on." We may hear that voice saying, "I need more quiet time. I need more space to breathe." After practicing yoga and meditation, we understand the key to inner peace: stillness, breath, yoga, and meditation. Once we know this, we want more of that; in fact, we want it all the time!

But the reality is that all the chaos and noise of life gets in the way! Then what? We get frustrated, which just compounds the issue. But does it get in the way or is it there for a reason? Aha!

I had an epiphany about all this and it was amazingly crystal clear. Life at home *is* our yoga practice. Our day-to-day reality *is* our yoga. Our family and all the challenges that come with them *is* our ultimate practice.

For a stay-at-home mom, every moment spent at home is a yoga practice. Practicing stillness and presence in each moment and in each chore is yoga. Everything we do is important to the totality of the life we have created. Nothing is mundane, although it may seem that way at times.

Every day offers us multiple opportunities to connect with our true Self, by feeling, speaking, or acting in a way that is more in alignment with who we truly are. The opportunity can present itself at work, balancing finances, or even listening to the news and examining how we perceive that information.

This is how simple it is to commit to a true yoga practice: Take five minutes several times a day to notice your breath and the calmness it creates. Take time to move at your desk or at home, just breathing or even simply stretching and removing tension from the body. Then get on with your day.

If we all ran to a mountain top or a cave for silence, we would find it. But can we maintain that silence and stillness and inner peace amidst the chaos of life? What we may wake up to is that the key to life is all around us now, in this moment—we don't need that mountain. Be silent and still while life is happening around you. Consider that your family and daily issues arise to help us recognize who our true, lovely Self really is.

Affirmations & Postures

Stretch your mind beyond what you thought possible. Let your reality shift to something you cannot even imagine.

Be present, notice when change and transformation is being offered, and then to leap toward it—letting go of fear, worry, and doubt.

Remember more than anything else that there is nothing as important as you feeling good as often as you can. Take time to assess where you are in your life; then define your intentions.

Stillness provides clarity which brings about joy.

Remember, we are all connected. Be kind to others, for in that moment we are showing kindness to ourselves.

Why is this continually happening for me? What am I to be learning? Where is the gift?" It's there; be open to receive it.

There are no more powerful words than "I am." Use them wisely.

Bridge

Chair

Childs

Downdog

Reverse Warrior

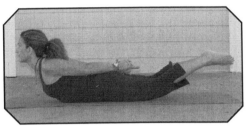

Locust

Tree

Warrior

Chapter 2
On Guilt versus Pleasure
Sacral Chakra: Svadhisthana

Yoga Practice

I still remember my first yoga class back in San Diego. Yoga came to me at a time when I was running five miles a day, working out at the gym early in the mornings, and partying really hard in the evenings. My friend took me to a yoga class early one Saturday morning and all I could think was, "This is ridiculously slow. When is the real movement going to begin?" When we got to final relaxation, Savasana, I couldn't sit still. I couldn't take it, even for five minutes! I laugh when I think about that now, as I scramble and hide to find stillness, peace, and quiet in my abundant days.

I remember the first time I really understood yoga. I actually heard my breath and moved with it! I looked forward to lying down in Savasana so I could reflect on how I felt. I memorized the pose sequences from my first yoga strength class so I could do them at home while my little ones were napping. I still remember the first time an "Om" got stuck in my throat as I chanted with everyone else. I didn't understand what I was feeling, but I knew it was the first step to a deep and everlasting shift.

My practice has changed and evolved into something so different from the way it was when I began over eleven years ago. I believe your yoga practice is so dynamic that it changes along with you as you grow. The funny thing is, once you do yoga, you can never leave it. It lives within you and permeates all aspects of your being whether you know it or not.

Yoga creates consciousness: it IS consciousness. It's mindful movement, enlightened awareness. Call it what you like, but yoga brings you to a state of being. The breathing, the moving, the quiet… it's an age-old tradition that has many forms. With the shift that is taking place on the planet right now, yoga really is the place to live.

The paradox is that once you become conscious, you can't go back to sleep. You may have periods of unconsciousness: when you get angry over something silly, when you worry about something you have no control over, or when you spend time wallowing in a past moment you can't change. But be-

yond that, the truth is that consciousness is always there. When you practice yoga on a regular basis, it becomes easier to access and simpler to recognize.

What happens when you find true consciousness? You become peaceful inside. You KNOW that all is well and that everything is moving into alignment for your highest good.

It only takes one yoga class and one conscious breath to find stillness. Yoga is the place to surrender and find stillness, peace, and new possibilities for your life ahead. Staying on the treadmill makes you tired, surrendering gives you peace.

Dream Big

I had the privilege of meeting Reverend Michael Beckwith and his wife Rickie Byars Beckwith at an event in Seattle, Washington, several years back. It was an amazing event for anyone interested in self-growth, contributing to global consciousness, and serving our nation. The message was: The powers of our thoughts create our reality. For those of you who don't know who Rev. Beckwith is, he is the spiritual leader and founder of The Agape Spiritual Center in Culver City, California. He has been featured in *The Secret* and he was on The Oprah Winfrey Show. His charisma delivers the important message of Oneness to anyone willing to listen.

When we put our mind to something, we have the power to create it. We all possess this power to create our life exactly as we intend. It's not hocus-pocus, it's not voodoo, it's reality. I know some may believe otherwise, but truthfully, our reality is what we make it.

Some may say, "Oh yeah? Well, I didn't choose to lose my job. I didn't choose to get divorced. I didn't choose to be in this situation." And to them I would say, "Not consciously you didn't." However, look at that situation and ask, "Was I happy in that job? Was I ready to evolve beyond that relationship?

Why was I so attached to that job, person, or material item? What can I do differently in my life now that I have this opportunity of time, space, stillness, and quiet"

In that space where change happens, you are offered the opportunity to slow down, take a look from outside, and say, "What do I want to create now?" The Universe has given you this gift and it's begging you to evolve! Somewhere in your consciousness, you were asking for this. "What now?" That's the scary part... the "what now?" But in stillness, the answers come to you easily.

We have the power to create the life we desire. It just takes intention, attention, and a willingness to let go. Be free from the negativity of other peoples' perceptions of the world. Be free from what you believe about yourself and the limits you have placed on yourself. Be free from the fear of change... all change is good.

Dream big! This is a time of miraculous change and transformation. Run into it if you are given the opportunity. Be free from the fear and the "what ifs." They don't do anyone any good.

One morning, my oldest daughter said, "You know, Mom, you should call Michael Beckwith and have him come and speak at the yoga studio. I bet he would feel so lucky to be there because it's so beautiful." Her eyes were so bright and open. She believed that he would come to the studio. And why shouldn't she? She has no one to tell her anything different.

Yes, they dream big. We all did when we were that little. Let's go back to that... it's way more fun than the alternative.

Living Your Dream

Have you ever wanted to do something for yourself and then decided at the last minute, "I better not," or thought "I shouldn't do this... I have so many other obligations I need to take care of first"?

We have all done it—put other people's needs first. If you're a woman, it's almost an inherent trait to put yourself last. But just for fun, dare I ask, why? Why do you continue to put everyone else's needs and desires before your own? Why do you continue to put your dreams on hold for your so-called "obligations" in life?

Ask yourself right now—what are your dreams and desires? What would the life of your dreams look like? This isn't some obligatory life that has been directed by your parents, teachers, or peers, but a life that is truly your own.

Do you even know what your dreams are? Or has it been so long that you have forgotten what they are?

The obligatory self-talk is what gets you to stop dreaming.

How could you leave your family, if only for a weekend, to follow a dream? How could you change jobs or move to another state to realize what living from your heart really felt like? Don't you owe it to everyone else to do what is "right?"

Who says what's right? How often do you allow others and society to make that decision for you? And when you finally do make the decision to follow a dream, why do you justify it? Why do you have to list the "reasons" why it's OK to do what makes you feel alive? Can't you just do something because it makes you happy?

And really, who are you justifying your actions to anyway? No one is listening.

You are justifying them to yourself.

Sure, pay the bills, stay home, go to work, get your degree—do whatever you aspire to do. But remember what is in your heart. Do it when the opportunity presents itself and don't justify it to anyone! Just say, because this sings to my heart! It's not selfish—it's your birthright to be happy and enjoy the love of life.

Think of life as one big opportunity. Be open to asking yourself, "Could I meet someone today who could transform my life? What opportunity could present itself if I choose this road?"

Personally, I have always been a risk taker. I like knowing that I have tried things without knowing what the outcome would be. Isn't that an exciting thought to imagine?

Keep in mind that transformation starts from within—not from without—and not because of others. Whether you have physical support to follow your dream or not, does not mean you can't do what you want to do. You always have Universal support. It all starts and ends with you. That's a challenging concept to surrender to, but it's true. You have the ability to dream; dream big and live large!

Take the leap—even if it is just for you! You deserve it!

Authenticity

What does that really mean? By definition, authenticity means truthfulness of origins, attributions, commitments, sincerity, and intentions. And I ask you now, how can you be authentic if you are living life in a state of unconsciousness? How do you know what you truly want or who you really are if you are living in state of uncertainty, judgment, parental fantasies, and ego-driven societal skepticism?

How do you know who you are authentically? Honestly, it's a tough road— first to realize authenticity and then to actually live it.

First, you must learn to be still long enough to hear the questions that are so important to the evolution of your soul: What is my purpose? What do I love? How can I grow? What is the meaning of the life I am living right now?

Then once you are able to "authentically" answer those questions, you may be fearful about going against the "norm." What will people think? What will this decision do for my current lifestyle?

I can tell you. It will open you up to more joy and creativity than you imagined. It will open doors you didn't expect to open. All because you had faith in that little voice telling you to move along!

But rest assured, you can't know what any decision will do for you in any moment except the moment you are in… that's authenticity. You are perfect right where you are! You can only know what you know. My grandmother used to say, "Wherever you go, there you are!" I used to think that was such a weird statement. Now I think she was very smart and insightful.

How's that for liberating? How can that be? Aren't you supposed to be "working on yourself?" What if I told you that you were perfect right now—in this moment? What if I told you that you were completely authentic according to your experiences right now? Would you believe me?

So if everyone is perfect right where they are, what's the point of learning more?

Because as long as you're still alive, there is more to learn. Period.

When your authenticity is challenged, the Universe is nudging you to evolve. Not change, not transform, evolve. You wake up to your thoughts, your actions, your perception, and you realize that your old thoughts just don't feel right anymore. You know what I'm talking about.

You're in a relationship or a job that just doesn't feel right anymore. You're living somewhere that is not speaking to your heart space. You say something to someone that is less than kind and you witness it happening.

That's when your soul is raising the bar. Your spirit is saying out loud, "Listen up, it's time to up the ante!"

Some of you may never experience this awakening, but everyone is offered the opportunity. The question is, are you able to hear it? Can you be still long enough to hear the call of your Soul? Move beyond the material, beyond the judgment, beyond the "should be's." The question is, when do you feel alive? And when you don't, do you cower and hide, or do you rise to the challenge and say, "Bring it on! I'm ready! What now?"

Go for the latter. It's not simple, but it is guaranteed to be more liberating and authentic.

Ah, there's that word again.

Which Thought Feels Better?

Want to change your life? Ask yourself this one question in moments when you notice your thoughts: "Which thought feels better?" Yes, it *is* that simple.

Life is impermanent—everything about life changes all the time. What do you do when the flow of life changes? Do you swim upstream against it or do you flow along with it and surrender to the process? Do you say, "I need to figure this all out so I can be happy again," or do you say, "I wonder where life is taking me now?"

Which thought feels better? One creates limits, tension and contraction. The other allows for space, openness, and expansion.

Contraction vs. expansion… which thought feels better?

What a wonderful time to find your true passion in life! Maybe right now you feel stuck, immobilized, and out of control. You're not; you are always in control of your perception. Maybe it's time for you to go inward and ask yourself important questions like, "What makes me happy?" and "What is available to me now?" The world holds infinite opportunities.

In yoga, we practice the art of presence in each posture. The intention for the asanas is to be steady and comfortable while maintaining continuity of breath. If you could find that same steady, comfortable posture in your thoughts and actions, then take a moment to ask yourself that quick question: "Which thought feels better?" Your life would change swiftly and dramatically.

If you are in the midst of change right now, if your life has turned upside down, and if you are looking for one mantra right now, let it be this: "I am open."

"I am open to the gifts this situation is giving me. I am open to the possibility that my life will be greater on the other side of this. I am open to change. I am ready to live my best life…. I am open."

Right now is a time of change. How fabulous are the gifts being presented to you now? If you can't find any, think harder. Look around you. They are there, waiting for you to notice them.

When you feel or think a negative thought, ask yourself which thought feels better, replace it with the complete opposite, and ask yourself again.

Breathe and become aware.

Waking Up

If you didn't already notice, there is an amazing shift in consciousness going on in our Universe. People are "waking up" from their unconscious lives and noticing they have opportunities to grow spiritually and actually live the joyful life they were born to live. They are realizing this through affirmative prayer, stillness, and meditation. They are realizing that the life they have been living is no longer serving them and they are being called to evolve.

Now, this may not be apparent. In fact, to some, it may look like something scary—a loss of a job, a loss of financial security, a divorce or other life altering experience. However, I invite you all to shift your patterns of thinking

just for today, so you may see the potential gift in our world situation and how it relates to your own personal shift.

If you don't know if this applies to you, see if you are asking questions like:

"Why is this happening to me? Why is the world doing this to me? How can this happen to me?" If you are, I soulfully ask you to read on.

Life is always changing. What we experience in any moment is just that, a moment. We aren't bound by the past, nor should we ever be afraid of the future.

In order for us to truly grow and evolve, we need to let go of the victim consciousness—the "poor me" mentality. We are not at the whim of the world; our joy does not come from the world—it comes from within and *only* from within.

If you are in a situation that seems negative, the question you should really ask yourself now is What is the meaning of this mess I am in? What is the meaning of the experience I have right now? Where can I grow in this situation? How can I evolve right now?

I promise you, you can radically change your life—in one lifetime, in one year, in one month—by changing your thinking.

Right now, there is nothing more important than taking the time to be still and completely present. You affirm that now is the time.

At the very least, please realize that your joy or happiness has nothing to do with what the world can give you—it's in you already. Your joy and greatest gifts are within you, waiting for you to announce them, to express them, to radiate them, to confirm them, and to live them in every area of your life.

I live mine by sharing yoga with those who are interested. I live mine by writing and listening to spiritual teachers who empower me with their words. I live mine by being present with my family and finding joy and love in even the darkest, scariest moments.

It's actually in those moments—when we notice the beauty and the love, despite the perceived fear—that we understand that there is a pristine presence around us. Our happiness is not linked to anything "working out." The presence of peace is just there, regardless of the "cards" life has handed us.

When you evolve into this place, the feelings of lack, limitation, and scarcity

can no longer vibrate with you. You have elevated your vibratory frequency and you have realized the world does not have to shift in order for you to be happy. One person cannot determine your happiness. You are empowered to find the joy that you deserve in that moment. Honestly, you only need to feel that presence one time. Once felt, that feeling will never go away.

Remember, you are empowered to be the best you can be because of your circumstances. Have fun in life. You are your best teacher. The world is your oyster right NOW.

Be empowered. Take charge of your life. Let go of being a victim. It's so much more fun being empowered!

Universal Guidance

I have heard many spiritual leaders say, "The Universe is conspiring every day for my highest good" or "The Universe has my back." I have always known that things happen for a reason, but to hear that the Universe has my back is much more visual and appealing to me.

For years I would pray when I wanted something to change or if I just wanted something. "Oh God, please help me get an A on tomorrow's test" or "Dear God, please let him ask me to the prom!"

Now I have come to realize, after years of reading, studying, and practicing yoga, that when we pray for something, someone, or an expected outcome to any circumstance, we are actually affirming that we don't have it, which means we are in a state of lack. This means we don't trust the Universe and we are just creating more of the same lack for ourselves.

Now, many years later, I finally understand Universal guidance. Instead of praying for something, I now say, "Allow circumstances to guide me to my

highest good."

There is so much faith and strength in that statement.

When you surrender to Universal guidance, you are essentially affirming that you are at peace with what is and that you know, beyond a shadow of a doubt, that this is what is meant to happen. Not only that, but if you perceive the circumstance to be negative, it may actually be your spirit moving you into the next stage of your evolution.

You may not understand that in the moment that it occurs, but you will most likely be able to look back and say, "Oh, of course that was supposed to happen."

Now, I'm not suggesting that you sit around and wait for happenstance to hand you your dreams on a silver platter. What I am saying is that setting clear and specific intentions about what you desire is important. You do this with your thoughts. A simple thought sets manifestation into motion immediately.

Then we put some of our attention on that which we desire. We talk about it, we read about it, we speak about it to others, we write about it. Once we really give it attention, we notice that the Universe begins giving us some of the same thoughts and/or experiences right back.

The most important step in this process is the third step: we let it go. This is where we surrender and have faith. We realize without a doubt, that we are on our journey, the path that we were meant to take. We have complete faith in things "working out." We know in the pit of our heart that everything showing up in our life is for our greater good—no matter what it may look like on the outside and no matter what other people may think.

Whatever you are going through right now, if there is chaos, upheaval, or uncertainty, understand that, beyond the shadow of a doubt, it is time to evolve. It is time to grow. Understand that the Universe wants to see you shine and the road there isn't always easy. Things may look different than you thought, but be open to the journey and what you will learn and become "on the other side."

Remember the Universe has your back—go for it and be open!

What Is

You have all heard the saying, "It is what it is," right? It's very familiar, but ask yourself if you accept this outlook on life. Do you agree that life is happening before your eyes and you have no say whatsoever in the direction it takes you? Or do you believe that there are some things that you obviously have some control over and some things that you just don't? Personally, I used to believe that we could change things in our lives just by setting goals to make a difference in situations that we were in. I think a bit differently now.

I heard a quote from Byron Katie and it hit me like a ton of bricks: "When we argue with what is, we create separateness, pain, and suffering for ourselves—and only 100 percent of the time."

Whoosh… wow. That's like a friendly slap in the face from the Universe. This statement relates a feeling to not accepting what is. Not accepting what is creates pain and suffering.

What's ironic about this is in the *Yoga Sutras*, Patañjali talks about how attachment to an outcome or expected result is the root of all suffering. Apparently this concept is not new. Then why do we keep suffering?

Imagine this: You have an expectation. Let's say you decide to take the day off work and go and pamper yourself. You are going to get a massage and then have lunch with friends. You are so excited to have a day just for you. At the last minute, someone calls and needs you. It could be that a coworker needs you at work or your child is sick. Whatever the situation, what is prevents you from having the day you planned for yourself.

How do you feel immediately? Disappointed, sad, frustrated, or angry—whatever the emotion, it's causing pain and suffering for you. Not only that, but you have been separated from everyone else. You have created space

between you and "them." Now your perception of this situation is all about you and not about the good for all. How would you feel if you simply accepted what is?

Visualize that same situation now, accept what is, free yourself from trying to control the situation or expecting a certain outcome, and allow the blessings from what is to just be. How much nicer does that feel?

Each of us forms expectations about our day, our week, and our life. It's good to have intentions, but expectations create limits and boundaries. Go into today with intentions, but let the day unfold before you. Allow what is to come to you naturally and freely. And notice the blessings in everything… remember, it's all FOR YOU.

Falling Into Your Fear…

You make amazing resolutions every year. You vow to make change. You KNOW at your core that life as you know it is NOT perfect. So why then, when you're faced with an opportunity to actually make a change, do you shy away from it? Why do you fall back into what is comfortable?

The way to live life is to fall into your fears. Face them and move past them. One of my dearest friends once said to me, "The way to the other side is not to move around all the tough times, but to dance through them." How awesome is that?

We all know that life hands us a deck of "cards" that represent circumstances and choices. You choose the road to take. By making decisions throughout your life, you create what you desire. Along that path, your desires may change and morph into something so completely different you may not recognize them at all.

However, your deepest sense of Self does recognize them, and connects with that yearning. You find yourself at a crossroads. Should you stay with what is comfortable or move in the direction of your heart? Move onto the road of evolution and grow into who you truly are at your deepest level of being.

Let's equate this concept to a yoga practice. Have you ever practiced a yoga pose and found yourself remaining comfortable in your version of the pose? For example, Eka Pada Rajakapotasana, Pigeon Pose. You remain in the variation that really isn't so challenging, but feels good. What if you went just a little bit beyond your comfort zone—not to a point of pain, but to a point of revelation—a point where you felt a new sense of openness in your body?

I know it's scary, but pushing yourself a little beyond your comfort zone may bring you to a new sense of openness, lightness, and space.

Imagine what life could be like if you actually faced your fears and moved beyond what you thought capable? Wow, what would that be like? I can tell you… liberating.

It's not easy to move past your fears, but once you get on the other side, life is vivid, in color, and real—a true representation of your spirit.

How many of you are living in that colorful world? According to statistics, only 15–20 percent of you. Most are living in the gray comfort zone.

Move past your fears. Move into the unknown. "There is nothing to fear except fear itself." What a profound statement from Franklin D. Roosevelt.

I invite each of you to name a fear and move past it. Maybe it's something simple, like trying a yoga class. Maybe it's making big change, like a new job, a new place to live, or a new relationship.

I invite you to drop into your fear and really see it for what it's worth… which is only a thought. A thought that you created to challenge yourself. That's right, you created it…no one else but you!

Change it, move past it, grow and transform. Find some space; the world is waiting for you and your gifts.

41

Non-Grasping... Non-Attachment

We form a society that relies on outside influences and environment. We rely on our schedule, our relationships, our job, and our material items. The downfall to this habit is that when change happens, we find ourselves lost. We may find ourselves blaming the outside world for the loss we have incurred. We may even have what some call an "identity crisis" when something changes in our world and shakes us to our core.

The *Yoga Sutras* discuss some amazing principles. However, aparigraha is the one we will examine to fully explain this amazing concept that our egos hold very dear.

Aparigraha is defined as "non-grasping." Your mind builds up ideas of how things "are" as a way of generating confidence and security for yourself. You may identify who you are by where you live, what job you hold, and who you associate with. This would be fine if life were indeed a stable event in which nothing ever changed, but life does change, and it encourages you to adapt and change along with it. The resistance to change and the need to hold onto things causes suffering and prevents you from living life open to the gifts you are to receive naturally.

Living with the knowledge that impermanence is your only constant will lead to less suffering and more awareness in your present moments. You are then more open to seeing the tombstones as stepping stones, the tornado as a clearing storm, and the upheaval as space for something new and exciting beyond your knowledge or imagination.

Your best security lies in releasing resistance and allowing yourself to grow, and becoming stronger and more resilient through that growth. You can live in the flow of life by letting go of the shore and letting the current take you.

Change

At the time I wrote these Oms, the economy was experiencing a huge shift. Banks were going under, massive amounts of people were losing their jobs, families were losing their homes, and people were basically being forced into a simpler life. This economic shift created fear for some, but for most, it was an opportunity to make change. For some, change feels good and for others, it's very scary.

The economy may have had something to do with the physical reality of this change. But dare I suggest that when things change, it's more about your perception of environmental influences? Could the feelings you feel in the midst of change actually be the attachment you feel to things staying the same? Could it be a fear of change within you? Whatever it is, according to Shakyamuni Buddha, the very nature of reality is impermanence and change.

Let me ask you: how do you feel when you go to the store and all the aisles have been changed around? Or when you come to yoga class one day and there is a new instructor? Or even worse, when someone takes your spot?

Ask yourself, "What is permanent?" Look to nature: the seasons, the Earth, and the ocean tides are constantly changing. Why should *you* stay the same?

Life is not a stable event in which nothing ever changes; life does change, and it encourages you to adapt and change along with it. The resistance to change and the need to hold onto things or people causes suffering and prevents you from living life fully and being open to the gifts you are to receive naturally.

What yoga philosophy and all the great Buddhist teachings tell us is that stability is a creation of the ordinary mind and that there isn't anything permanent in our lives that we can indeed hold onto. When we live with the

knowledge that impermanence is our only constant, we will experience less suffering and more awareness in our present moments.

Holding onto ideas, material items, or even individuals can lead to the destruction of those very things we most value. Our best security lies in releasing resistance to change, allowing ourselves to grow, and becoming stronger and more resilient through that growth.

When things in our lives are in upheaval or are changing around us, it is the Universe preparing us for something greater beyond our knowledge. When we resist change or hold onto the sameness, we are actually limiting ourselves to what is comfortable.

I love this saying: "My actions are my only true belongings. I cannot escape the consequences of my actions. My actions are the ground on which I stand."

Think about a time in your life when you were resistant to change. How did that make you feel? Evaluate how much you hold onto to feel secure. What would happen if you let go? What would be the worst case scenario? How could it benefit you?

Be a Giraffe

Did you know that the giraffe has the longest neck and the biggest heart of any mammal on Earth?

From an anatomical standpoint, it's obvious why the heart is so big. The blood sure has a long way to travel to get to the brain! But let's look at this a little more thoughtfully.

The giraffe is the tallest mammal on Earth. This lucky mammal has an aerial view of everything. He can see things from an elevated perspective. Imagine how clear things are to him. Wouldn't it be amazing to be able to see yourself from above—to watch the way you communicate, react, and deal with life?

You can begin to understand this when you meditate and practice yoga on a regular basis. You can't help but see yourself in a different light. You may even realize that you don't have to be IN life, but you are only a PART OF life.

Interesting, isn't it?

Now let's take the big heart thing. According to the chakras, the heart chakra is full of compassion, joy, love, and forgiveness. Here is an animal that not only sees things from high above and witnesses clarity, but that also sees things with compassion, joy, forgiveness, and love. What would it be like to witness clarity in our lives and realize we aren't our lives, but only a part of them? To watch our lives like a movie and accept that we are only a small part of the Universe? To release the responsibility we feel about how our life plays out? It would be wonderful to actually witness life going on around us without trying to control it and make it into what we think it's supposed to be. It would be wonderful to actually watch our life from above and not be in the midst of it.

What would it look like to view everything with compassion and joy? Everything! We would see it because we were up high instead of buried under it. We would know that everyone around us was on the same path of living happily. We wouldn't be so quick to assume or judge that maybe they were out to get us. We wouldn't allow what they were doing to affect us so much because we would realize that it was all part of the plan. How would we be living if we lived with a big heart like the giraffe? Blissfully comes to mind.

Know that when you begin your yoga practice you may be in it: living in the midst of life. But when you commit to a consistent yoga practice, you become more like the giraffe. There's more clarity, more openness, and more compassion.

Take a chance—try being a giraffe. It's fun being tall and in love with the Universe!

The Mirror of My Self

Ever experience people in your life who really get under your skin? For some reason they just bug the heck out of you. You just KNOW that they are out to bother you on purpose. You wish they would just leave you alone already!

What if I told you I have the perfect plan on how to never let them bother you again? It would require you to be open to a potentially new concept… are you ready to hear it?

The secret is this: those people are, in some capacity, reflections of you. How can I say this? Because if we believe and know that we are all just energy, if we believe and accept that we are here to grow and evolve into our highest Self, if we can believe and recognize that we create our own reality, if we can surrender to the simple mantra of yoga which is we are One, then it would ONLY make sense that we create each life circumstance AND we draw the people into our lives who will allow us the opportunity to SEE that side of ourselves.

How does that statement make you feel?

You might be thinking, "I don't believe that, not even one bit." If you are feeling this way, I caution you, someone else will come along in your life, or another circumstance will happen to you that will reflect this lesson again and again until you see it.

You see, the Universe basically caresses you with an idea. If you are blind to the messages, then it might gently tap you with the same idea in a different situation. When you deliberately continue to ignore the message, one day the Universe just slaps you upside the head and says, "Why aren't you listening to me?" This can cause a lot of suffering and pain, so remember, we are here to be happy. We are here to grow.

Now, when those annoying people do the same thing to you, why not take a breath, look at them, and ask yourself, What is bothering me about them? Notice the sensations in your body. For example, you are feeling aggression. No matter how kind you are, these people are still aggressive in their speech and actions toward you. Next time, breathe in a breath of compassion for them, while saying (in your mind, of course), I forgive you for taking out your personal aggression on me.

You know what you have done in that very moment? Not only have you allowed compassion and empathy to flow through you to them, but you have also opened up a little space for you to see and feel differently. With this new awareness, pay attention to times when you display similar aggression. Consistently practicing this technique allows you to look at yourself compassionately, so you can move beyond these negative feelings in your own life and minimize the instances when you experience them.

Is this making sense?

Now remember, we agreed that we are all One, right? So if we are all One, this makes complete sense. Forgive and love your neighbor as you would forgive and love yourself. Forgive and love yourself as you would forgive and love your neighbor.

There are no coincidences in life! We create everything that allows us to learn and grow, especially those difficult circumstances, challenging times, and annoying people. Open up to the possibility that the Universe offers all perceived negativity as a growing experience.

Next time you come across people who pull at your energy negatively, open up—have compassion for them and you will heal yourself. I promise.

Judgment

Have you ever judged anyone? Instinctively, your first answer might be "no," but subconsciously the answer is *always* "yes." Let me give you an example. I am driving my kids to school one morning, and we stop at a light. I notice the man next to me eating a fast food cheeseburger. I say out loud, "OH MY! WHY is that man eating a cheeseburger? He shouldn't be eating that first thing in the morning!"

From out of nowhere, my oldest daughter, then six years old says, "Mommy, you know, everyone has their own thing. He can make his own choice." I literally lost my breath. I said, "You know, you're right, honey. I wonder why I would have said that." And she said, "Well, Mommy, you just want everyone to be healthy, but everyone has their own idea about what healthy is." This, out of the mouth a six-year-old.

So I said, "You're absolutely right, honey. I should not have judged him. It's really not my business." To this, she replied, "That's right, Mommy. There is your business, his business, and God's business, and that was definitely HIS business."

My younger one, then three, whose favorite words were "me too," had to pipe in and be heard. She leaned toward the center of the back seat, looked at me in the rearview mirror, and said, "Yes Mommy—that really didn't sound so nice."

I was called out—big time. That was one of my proudest moments as a mother.

This brings to mind two things for me. First, there are three types of business: your business, my business, and God's business. And when you're in anyone else's business but your own, who is minding yours? Thank you Byron Katie by the way.

The second thing (which can be comforting or daunting) is your kids are listening. You may not think they hear you, but they do. I think I mentioned that statement about businesses and minding your own <u>one time</u>!

It is also important to understand that we are a judging society. We judge EVERYTHING. We can't help it, but we can limit it—drastically.

Does this mean we have to be perfect? No way! In fact, it's better not to be perfect. That way our kids won't think they have to be perfect. We are humans, remember? Be compassionate with yourself as you transcend human behavior. Be ready, be yourself, wake up to your words and thoughts, and judge no one—start with yourself.

I Love

Closing my yoga studio in our little community of Vancouver, Washington, awakened me to many life lessons that I would have never experienced had I not been through that huge loss.

It's true that in times of loss, we really do break through to the other side of who we are and we are then able to share our little light with the world. We may never be able to do this if we don't experience loss or grief.

Something I have always believed in, even as a young adolescent, was to always, always do what you LOVE—not what you feel obligated to do, not what your parents tell you should do, not what society says you can make a lot of money doing. DO WHAT YOU LOVE.

LET GO of the "I should" and instead choose "I love."

How many times have you been afraid of what other people would think when you make decisions like this? How many times have you allowed your

fear of judgment to influence your choices about where you live, if you go to college, who you marry, if you stay home with your kids, if you go to work, or your job or career path? I can tell you that fear influences your choices almost all the time.

But remember, you have a gift to give. You chose life because you have something to share and give of yourself that will benefit the world in some way. And guess what, NO ONE knows what that is except YOU.

We are offered opportunities to make thousands of decisions every single day—thousands. We may not take time to evaluate some decisions; we just react and make them. But with other decisions, we may experience internal guidance.

That internal guidance may come to you in a little voice that says "Is that REALLY what you want to do?" The voice usually touches your heart. Think Glinda the Good Witch in The Wizard of Oz..

Alternatively, you may hear, "Really? THAT'S what you want to do? What will people think?" That voice would be the Wicked Witch of the West cackling at you. Remember the witch who had a green face, long nose, and ended up melting at the end of the movie?

The question is, which voice do you want to listen to? Glinda speaks from your heart. The road you choose with Glinda may be more difficult at times (remember all those lessons Dorothy had to learn along the yellow brick road?), but in the end you come back to yourself just like Dorothy went back to Auntie Em.

In our lives, we may have to weather a tornado or two in order to live authentically. We may have our home or the "movie" of our life ripped out from underneath us.

We may find ourselves in a strange land just like Dorothy did, but the lessons in those times of perceived despair are really songs of our heart begging us to shift and not be afraid.

Don't be fearful of judgment. Allow yourself to hear the voice of Glinda— that's your heart. Life is too short to make decisions based upon fear… go for what you love! It proves to be fulfilling every single time.

Peace and Abundance in Uncertainty

Remember that life is always changing, so we will also change and experience uncertainty at some point. How can we find peace in those moments? Our first feeling in times of uncertainty is usually fear because we don't know what is going to happen next. It's like walking around in the dark.

So to find peace in those moments, recognize the fear first. Surrender to it. Then the abundance in what is will manifest naturally.

What happens when life creates a movie for you that you don't exactly understand? Life is really unpredictable, isn't it? Unpredictability can create fear for most, right? Fear is OK as long as you don't remain in your fear. Fear can be helpful if you recognize it and move past it.

Ask yourself if you like the movie of your life. Are you stuck in fears of what is to come? Are you noticing questions like "what if?" or "what now?" or "what's next?" If so, take a breath and surrender to the fear.

Create peace, calm, and stillness; notice the beauty of what is happening in your life right now. Surrender to it and really see it. Every single situation CAN have beauty and opportunity if you choose to be still and notice the beauty instead of the uncertainty. After that stillness, surrender happens naturally; you see an opening: a door or bright light.

You may not know what living a life aligned with your passions looks like at any given moment. But the beauty in that is knowing and recognizing that you are the conscious co-creator of your life. Your perception is what creates the movie you are watching. You can create exactly what you want for yourself. Start now—get quiet and clear. It's all right there waiting for you: abundance, joy, and peace within.

Redirect

Have you ever stubbed your toe while you were in a hurry to do something? Have you tripped, dropped something, or hurt yourself while you were on your way to getting angry and frustrated about a situation you were in?

I'm sure some, if not most of you, can relate to this, but have you asked yourself why that happens? I can tell you. It's a subtle message from the Universe telling you to either slow down and change the reaction, or live in the moment.

Think about it. You wake up, late for work. You immediately jump from the bed, only to stub your toe on the bedpost. You angrily continue to move to the shower, thinking, "Great, so THIS is how my day is going to be."

You get out of the shower, not even fully dressed yet, and you realize the dog has pooped in your room again, one child is naked and crying because she can't find her skirt, the other child is complaining about something you can't understand, there is unfolded laundry, a list of things you still have to do, and messes in nearly every room in the house.

Sound familiar?

You may immediately feel unsettled, frustrated, tired, and maybe even angry. You go to grab a cup of coffee, but while you pour your coffee, it spills all over the counter. You think, "I knew that was going to happen." You begin to spiral into negative thoughts that will follow you for the rest of your day unless you stop them.

Want to hear a liberating statement? You are not responsible for anything but your thoughts and reactions.

Think about that for a moment.

Rewind back to when you stubbed your toe. By thinking negatively about

this natural event, you suffer. You manifest the trials and tribulations of your upcoming day by perpetuating the negative feeling. What happens is you get more of the same.

What would happen if you took that message as a sign to stop, breathe, and take just one minute of stillness before going forward? What might happen then? Think about it for a moment. That one minute could change your entire day!

Now let's say you missed that message and kept going, spiraling down, thinking about your horrible day to come. The next message would be the dog pooping, child crying and complaining, pick one—any of them are signs. It could be a sign to stop, listen, be present, and notice the beauty here. Live IN this moment… it will never come again. There could be beauty and laughter here, you know. Maybe when you think about it later, you might even laugh—a surefire sign that it's not that important.

But let's say you didn't notice those signs. You just got more frustrated because your mind started going to the laundry, the homework, the lunches, the snacks to pack… agh! NOW you've spilled your coffee. That's it!

That was the sign that would either push you over the edge OR allow you to realize… there it is. The Universe finally slapped you upside the head and said, "That's ENOUGH! SLOW DOWN ALREADY! Take a breath, for goodness' sake!"

Interesting, isn't it?

So I say to you now, if you don't know what to believe, believe in the Universe conspiring for your highest good all the time. Remember, it gives you signs. You may not totally understand the signs, but work toward being more present when they happen.

Stubbing your toe or any other action that stops you dead in your tracks is usually a sign to take notice. Slowing down, changing your reaction, or noticing the beauty can create a much more wonderful feeling than spiraling into negativity.

Remember, you are only responsible for your thoughts and reactions—nothing else. Take care of them in the most present way possible.

Just Rake the Sand

I had the opportunity to travel to Jamaica, where I spent an entire week resting and reflecting. It's amazing what your mind comes up with in times of stillness with absolutely no distractions and nothing to do.

I noticed a couple of things about the Jamaicans. One was their sense of seemingly genuine happiness. I laughed because I would ask them, "How come you are always smiling?" Their response every time was, "Because mon, life is good." It didn't matter if I asked the bartender, the manager, or the guy cleaning the pool. Every person I talked to was simply happy. And I wondered why.

Through this inquiry, I sadly realized that Americans have a hard time achieving this same happiness. We walk briskly, always in a hurry, with determined looks on our faces and phones in our ears and then wonder why we aren't happy. I'll tell you one reason: We are never in the present moment. We are always thinking about what we have to do later or what we didn't do earlier.

Jamaicans understand presence. They understand the Now. They aren't thinking about yesterday or tomorrow. It's all about the Now. Of course, it helps to have sun almost every day, but that's another story.

The other thing that really struck me was the simplicity of their lives. I watched one of my new Jamaican friends rake the sand. Yes, rake the sand. Every morning, at 6 a.m., he showed up and organized the beach chairs in perfect rows, cleaned up all the glasses and towels left from the night before, and then began to rake the sand. The lines he made in the sand were perfect. It was mesmerizing to watch.

He obviously took pride in his work. I kept thinking about how we sometimes complain about what we "do" for a living or how many times we have

taken shortcuts just to get our tasks done so we can go home. I realized, as I watched him every morning, how important his work was to him and how much pride he had in what he "did." Every person I met in Jamaica was like that— prideful and happy that they were doing what they loved to do and were doing it well.

Sometimes we think we have to do big things to make a big difference in the world. We work really hard, we jeopardize our health, and we sacrifice time with family—all to make a "difference" or make the "big bucks."

If you really think about it, it's our smaller contributions that actually make bigger differences. It's things like making our house a home, putting effort into playing with our kids, deciding to adopt a dog or a cat, or how we cut our lawn. Those little things really make big differences in the world.

We don't need to go out and "prove" ourselves by working so hard we can't see straight anymore. We just need to do something as simple as rake the sand and do it well.

My trip to Jamaica brought me back to the importance of presence and the simplicity of life that we all forget about as we move quickly and furiously toward… what again?

Ask yourself today: Did you take time to see something simple? Did you take time to smile? Did you laugh at something or sing a happy song? Try turning off your phone and not checking e-mail for a day… wow, what a time saver! Do it—it's really all you need.

Living Passionately

Finding passion in life can be a daunting task. We are hesitant to take the "plunge" toward something we love. Why? We feel fear, obligation, or perhaps self-doubt. We have false ideas, concepts, and beliefs about our own abilities and the world around us. We remain stagnant in our roles because it's easier than jumping off a cliff to live our passion.

In the face of what seems like scarcity, great ideas are born! Opportunity abounds for individuals who have the insight to notice that. Perception is everything!

According to a 2005 study, only 20 percent of Americans are happy with what they are doing in life. That means that only one in five Americans is happy. Would they have realized they weren't happy if the Universe hadn't shifted so exponentially that they had to ask themselves what they were made of at their core? If nothing would have changed in their lives, would they have just kept trotting along on life's treadmill until one day, maybe at retirement, they realized, "Wow, I just spent 30 years of my life doing something that did not make me happy at all. How did I get here?"

Self-inquiry is noticing your thoughts, asking where they are coming from, letting go of blame and going within, then creating thoughts to better fit your desired outcome. This is where living passionately ignites. This is where your life begins. This is where we awaken to who we truly are.

I believe that this awakening can start with a dedicated yoga practice. When you are still, you begin to notice the movie of your life. You can then decide if you are satisfied or if you want something different.

Start asking yourself these big questions: Do I LOVE my life? Do I LOVE what I do? What if I could be, do, or have ANYTHING? What would it be? Is it present in my life now? When I am living my most ideal life, I AM… Finish that last sentence with answers about your career, your relationships, your finances, your lifestyle, and your environment. Then ask yourself, "Am I doing those things? Do I have those things? Am I those things? No? Why?"

That's where it gets tricky. Answers almost always come up as: I have a family to feed. I have an obligation to my kids. I can't possibly do that; I wouldn't make enough money.

The reality is that there is only one obligation you have in life and that is to be happy. Coming from the heart of a mother, and speaking to those of you with children, this can sound a bit backward. But truly ask yourself, who matters most? Are you really any good to anyone if you are cranky and miserable? What example do you want to set for your kids? To fulfill the needs of others first and *then* take care of yourself? Or do you want to show them the importance of living a life of fulfillment?

Are you just waiting for the day that you can do what you want to do? If you nodded, please understand that your day is now. The present moment is waiting for you to decide. Do you want to keep doing what you are doing or are you ready to change the movie of your life? Begin by being still and listening to your heart—your heart is where truth resides.

Limiting beliefs will follow you around forever if you don't question them. You don't need to dig through years of issues to try and "figure it all out." Just look at the present moment and ask yourself, Is this where I want to be? If so, GREAT! If not, find some stillness and get some clarity.

Realizing all of these things represents so much: change, transformation, opportunity, new ideas, concepts, and beliefs. The world is your oyster.

The Trampoline

A few years back, I attended a four-year-old's birthday party at a local gymnastics facility. Originally I was going to stay home and get some work done while I sent my then husband out to do the "birthday thing." I consciously considered my new intention which was—to have FUN—and changed my mind at the very last minute.

Normally at kids' birthday parties, I stand on the sidelines just watching my daughters, offering a "Nice job honey!" or "WOW! Good for you!" But this time I thought, "No, I am going to have FUN."

I decided to start with the trampoline. All these little kids are jumping and laughing and having the time of their lives. Why can't I?

Let me ask you, have you ever jumped on a trampoline? I'm not talking about when you were a kid; I'm talking recently. It's so stinking fun! Now imagine adding a springboard that can catapult you into a pit of foam blocks! Try that! What a rush!

So now, I'm having a blast with my youngest daughter on the trampoline. We're having so much fun that she is laughing so hard she gets the hiccups. I glance over at my other daughter and she is swinging from the trapeze and tossing herself into the foam pit. Last week she was terrified of this, so I am very proud, but also intrigued.

My youngest goes off with her friends and I decide to try the trapeze. I feel that I am going beyond my old self who would have been worried about what other people were thinking. After a try or two, I toss myself into the pit and laugh like crazy!

After participating in the fun, I get caught up in kid energy. I notice myself becoming a little girl again. I get on another trampoline and start bouncing. I call my friend over and say, "You have GOT to try this!" We are on the trampoline and I am cracking up, watching her hair get all crazy and knowing that I look terribly silly.

I have an epiphany: Wouldn't it be great if every workplace had one of these? Better yet, what if there was a gymnastics class for adults? But the class format wouldn't be focused on physical fitness; it would be more about releasing the mental garbage from our day.

I couldn't help but think how great it would be if it were mandatory for every company to have a trampoline room. Whenever you felt stressed, you could walk into a room that had only a trampoline and wall-to-wall mirrors. All you could do was jump and watch yourself. What a crack-up! You couldn't leave that room until your attitude totally changed. Wouldn't that be awesome?

So for those of you who are laughing right now—LAUGH! For those of you who aren't and don't get it, go find a trampoline and jump. And don't stop until you laugh!

Tight in a Bud

I love this quote from Anaïs Nin: "And the time came when the risk to remain tight in a bud was more painful than the risk it took to blossom."

How many of you feel "tight in a bud?" Maybe you're just waiting for the economy to turn around and THEN you can make a difference. Or you're waiting until your partner finishes their degree/career climb and THEN you can go for what you love and are passionate about. Maybe you are waiting until your kids go off to college, then YOU will have your turn. Or maybe you're letting the clock tick, waiting to retire. After all that time working and waiting, waiting, waiting, you will DEFINITELY do what you love because THEN it will be your time.

Guess what? NOW is your time to blossom. We are our life. There's no "waiting in line" to get where we want to go. The time is NOW!

Every life experience we are having is one we are meant to have so we can ask the questions:

How can I serve? How can I grow? What can I celebrate?

The experiences we have may not always be gift-wrapped or handed to us on a silver platter. In fact, most of the time, our more challenging and difficult experiences offer us the highest growth, most abundance, and the greatest pristine beauty. They offer us a chance to see ourselves as we truly are. Most often, they offer us the opportunity to notice those angels around us who have been there all along waiting for us to ask those powerful questions.

During difficult and challenging times, we are not meant to sit around and wallow in our "victim mentality." In fact, no one is ever a victim—we are simply offered opportunities throughout our lives to choose to remain tight in a bud or to blossom into what we are meant to be.

Ask yourself, "What is happening in my life that could be misconstrued as challenging?" Then ask yourself, "Did I ask for this situation or circumstance?" By the way, the only answer to that is yes. I know that's hard to hear, but it's true! Then ask yourself, "How can I serve in this situation?" "How can I grow and what can I celebrate?"

Always, without a doubt, you will find something that urges you to blossom. Why stay tightly wound when you can bloom so beautifully? When you see springtime in all its glory, imagine those gorgeous flowers as part of you… because they are.

Pulling Up the Roots

Spring brings transformation, growth, renewal, and rebirth. One spring I was outside digging a hole to plant my rosebush and had an amazing realization. As I began to dig the hole, I came across a complex system of roots. Big roots—the ones you have to cut to get past so you can find some healthy dirt. It probably took me an hour just to get through the roots.

Once I got past the roots, I came across a bed of river rocks. Not as easy to move, but with a little elbow grease and cajoling, I pulled the rocks from the hole.

During this process, when I got beyond my back hurting and my arms getting sore, I realized a few things. One was how long those roots had been there. My guess was a very long time. I did my best to treat them with kindness, feeling compassion for whatever tree or bush they belonged to. Another thing that came to mind was those rocks. I could have been terribly frustrated with the rocks, but instead I found space for gratitude because my kids love painting rocks! So now I had an entire pile of rocks for them to paint!

I turned that into a metaphor. That hole could be equated to how you perceive or function in your life. How many times do you set out to do something simple, like enjoy your day with simplicity, only to be faced with a system of roots or a wall of rocks? Get it?

How do you handle those roots or rocks? Using the metaphor, you could simply plant your rosebush on top of the roots or rocks but that could eventually kill the bush, since it doesn't have a clear pathway to grow properly. You could move to another area of your yard, but you picked this spot. And who knows what lies underneath that other pile of dirt? Not only that, but every time you looked at that bush, you would remember that you compromised what you truly wanted because the effort to dig was just too much.

Affirmations & Postures

Spring is magical but you have to go through fall and winter to get there.

Strive to be happy—that is all that matters.

You have the ability to dream; dream big and live large! Take the leap—even if it is just for you! You deserve it!

I am open to the gifts this situation is giving me. I am open to the possibility that my life will be greater on the other side of this. I am open to change. I am ready to live my best life... I am open.

Remember the Universe has your back—go for it and be open!

You can live in the flow of life by letting go of the shore and letting the current take you.

Life is too short to make decisions based upon fear... go for what you love! It proves to be fulfilling every single time.

Anahata

Bow

Bridge

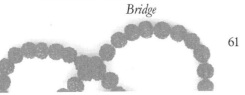

Cat

Dancers

Cobra

Frog

Lunge

Sidebend

Chapter 3
On Shame versus Personal Power
Solar Plexus Chakra: Manipura

Do You Let Fear Stop You?

I took my girls to get their ears pierced one spring— what a learning experience that was for us all! We were the first ones there, which was nice—no waiting in line with anticipation.

My older daughter, Isabella, who was 6 at the time, went first. My three year old, Ava, and I watched her sit in the chair. We kept telling her how brave she was, how awesome it would be, and how sparkly her ears were going to look. Now, you may be thinking, "Why did you have Ava sit there and watch?" I asked myself the same thing the second the two ladies at Claire's stuck the earrings into Isabella's ears.

Childhood memories of my own ear piercing came flooding back to me when I saw the look on Isabella's face. She looked like someone had pulled the rug out from underneath her. Her eyes got huge and tears began springing from them. As I held Ava's hand and cuddled Isabella to my chest, all I could think of was how I was going to get Ava into that chair. Isabella was crying out of shock, and Ava was crying out of fear. We were quite a sight.

There was a mother and her daughter waiting behind us; the mother was smiling empathetically at me. At this point, Ava was crying incredibly loudly, but Isabella had been given a sucker for being so brave. Things were looking up!

We let the girl waiting behind us go next so we could talk for a little about the experience. I am so in love with my girls—they are so "awake" and have so much to say. Ava was still crying, her face red, tears streaming down her cheeks. I asked her, "Do you want to go next?" She wailed loudly, "I do, mommy, but I am so scared now!"

And I thought, Well, of course she is. Who wouldn't be? So I said, "We can wait and come back another day if you want." Through her sobs she said, "Mommy, I really, really, really want to get my ears pierced today but I think I am just too scared."

My heart seriously leapt out of my chest.

I realized that my daughter was having an internal dialogue with herself as I sat there and witnessed it.

Not only that, but I had to ask myself: how many times do we, as adults, adolescents, teenagers, and parents have the same internal dialogue with ourselves about other issues bigger than getting our ears pierced? How many times are we offered the opportunity to take the next step in our lives and we are immobilized by fear— fear of the unknown, fear of others judging us, fear of making the wrong decision, fear that it will hurt?

It's ok to be a little fearful of the unknown—that's normal. But the bigger question to ask yourself is: Is this fear that is immobilizing me my own fear, someone else's fear, or is it an unrelated fear from a past experience that is irrelevant in this situation?

We base our actions on old stuff. Fear is almost always irrational, based on irrelevant information. So go with your gut, let your heart lead, and move beyond the hurt. Don't let fear stop you from listening to your heart and participating in life.

Be the Leader of Your Life

There is tranquility in just sitting and being, recognizing each moment for what it has to offer. Being in the moment can be scary sometimes because big questions usually arise in that stillness. Why am I here? What is my purpose?

What if I don't have a purpose? Is this the life I chose? What am I meant to be doing? Why can't I just sit still?

Most of you busy yourselves with so much drama, material items, open-ended plans, and unnecessary issues. Really, how much time do you spend inside? How much time do you spend just being?

At a seminar I attended a few years back, Michael Beckwith said, "You are the leader you have been waiting for." Think about that for a minute. We spend so much time outside ourselves, don't we? We look to the world and ask what it can give us. We look to other people to make us happy. We expect material objects to fulfill our need for completion. We crave love, appreciation, and recognition from others around us. When really, the only place we can look for anything is inside.

Inner peace and happiness is found within, not without. Material objects are nice—we can enjoy the fun of physical manifestation! But they're empty when we expect things or people to bring us happiness and joy. Loving ourselves must come first before we can truly love another. This is truth.

You are the only one who truly knows which road to take, which mountain to climb, and which wave to ride. But how many times do you follow others? How many times do you allow the perceptions and opinions of others decide how you feel, respond, or react? How many times do you allow others to lead your life?

As a parent, sometimes I mistakenly believe that I am the leader of my children, but really I'm not. I'm just here to hold up signposts along the way, offering them the space to find the leaders within themselves.

Ask yourself: What do I believe? What do I want to do? What makes me happy and content? Let the voice inside become louder and clearer than the voices and opinions on the outside. Trust yourself and live your own perception— regardless of what other people say or think.

Be the leader of your life that you have been waiting for. Only you know the answers. Believe me, when you stop leading others and just lead yourself, your life becomes a true manifestation of who really are and even better, who you are becoming.

Spiritual Warrior

What does it mean to become your own Spiritual Warrior, anyway?

It means recognizing the qualities within yourself that are the innate gifts you were born with and expressing them full out—without fear of being judged. It means knowing the qualities within you that keep you from realizing your most authentic self, blessing them one by one with compassion and then replacing them with qualities that serve you better. It means visualizing your Self, every day, as you know your soul to be: full of love, light, harmony, compassion, joy, and gratitude for life as you see it right Now.

Being a Spiritual Warrior also means committing to your practice, whatever that may be. It may be yoga practice, meditation, attending church, reading a book, being one with nature, eating healthy, exercising, talking less, or listening more. Being a Spiritual Warrior means challenging yourself to be more, do more, and experience more. On the other hand, it could mean to be less, do less, and experience less, too. We all have a Spiritual Warrior inside of us waiting to be birthed so she can express herself completely!

Being a Spiritual Warrior means navigating through your dense layers of consciousness with awareness and resilience. It means venturing out with excitement and experiencing life's challenges and growing pains. It means looking life in the face and saying, "I'm ready!" It means looking at yourself honestly and saying, "There is room to grow. There is room to learn. How can I transcend and be all that I am meant to be?" It's asking the bigger questions in each moment as you move through layers of consciousness. It's noticing your reactions and responses and making changes instantly so you are more of a reflection of your Self.

DANA DAMARA

Being a Spiritual Warrior isn't always easy. It requires patience, forgiveness, compassion, generosity, integrity, honesty, commitment, and persistence.

Ask yourself today: What am I willing to do differently in order to reflect my Spiritual Warrior within? What am I willing to do today that requires a bit of risk on my part? Which parts of my ego am I willing to part with in order to birth those parts inside me that are waiting to speak up and be heard?

As Michael Beckwith says, "The longer you hide out in the attempt to remain safe, the more you become fearful, nervous, hesitant. You will not be present as a participant in birthing a new world, a world that very much needs and wants the contribution of your consciousness." Don't wait for tomorrow to be all that you can be. Participate in life—grow, change, transform, and be the change you wish to see.

Live Full Out.

Dropping the Ego

It's fun to contemplate your ego and its role. You know the ego: that voice that steers you in the direction of self-preservation, recognition, survival, and the physicality of life. I invite you to begin reflecting on the moment(s) in time when you notice the ego acting out. That voice is so damn loud!

In those moments, if you listen with intention, you can hear a timid voice in the background that says, "Wait a minute…that doesn't vibe with me." That's your heart and it may be faint and quiet. In fact, it may be so quiet, you may not even be sure you heard anything at all. It's been trying to speak up, but you haven't heard it. It's even taken a back seat on purpose because it loves you so much. But once you really hear it, you will always hear it.

70

You hear it, you notice it, but do you take action based on its guidance? Maybe not right away, but once you hear that voice, that quietly confident voice, you can't really ever ignore it. To be fair, it's easier to listen to your ego. You have been listening to it your entire life, so why change now?

Because now is the time to awaken—that's why.

It's time to awaken to that inner guidance system that lights the way to empowerment, evolution of your soul, enlightenment, spiritual liberation, authentic self— whatever you call it. That little voice brings you back to your heart, where we all began before societal "charm" and parental fantasies created grooves in our thinking and our patterns of behavior.

How do you disembark from the ego train and live from your heart? It's exciting to know that science proves that you can change the patterning in your brain. You actually can rewire old thoughts, belief systems, and ways of doing things. Understanding and accepting this is the first step to waking up. Being kind and compassionate when you don't listen or notice the ego until later is another important aspect of the evolution of your heart.

But most importantly, you listen. You become still in as many moments throughout the day as you can. You ask yourself: How does it feel when I say this, think this, do this? How does this feel?

You ask yourself, moment to moment: What is my motivation in making this decision? Is it to gain recognition or celebrity? To exude power over another? To be heard? To be right no matter what?

These are signs that you are working from your ego. The ego wants all those things so it can survive.

However, the heart space wants love, forgiveness, gratitude, inner peace, and serenity. Ask yourself if your intention is to make a silent difference, to serve, to love, to elevate another's self worth, or to simply make someone happier than when you saw them. That is the heart.

What is my motivation? That's a huge question in making any decision—ask what your motivation or intention truly is. If it's "to help people," for example, or "to make a difference in my community"—dig deeper. These are unconscious motives that have more meaning to them. What's behind that motivation? Dig deep.

I once read that character means "the imprint on the Soul" and that persona means "a mask worn by actors." It would seem to me that character means living from your heart, listening to that voice. Living from your ego would mean living a mediocre life—one that sustains you but doesn't transcend you.

You connect with your character in your choices if you recognize your deep, conscious motivations. You can live from that place when you are still and listen intently with discipline and dedication. Do you live from that space every single time? Most likely not—you are a spiritual being living a human experience. But when you incorporate meditation, yoga, affirmative prayer, or daily quiet contemplation into your life, you can. You awaken—and what a beautiful world it truly is.

The Law of Opposites

I attended a yoga class recently, and the instructor was very focused on grounding ourselves in our postures so we could ultimately become lighter. For 90 minutes, I kept hearing her voice telling me to ground and feel the essential lightness shining from within me.

How brilliant, I thought. And then, of course, it got me thinking about the law of opposites. How can we really know lightness until we feel grounded? How can we know pure joy without suffering? How can we display courage without fear? What about true compassion and love without grief?

I sometimes find myself protecting my kids from sadness, fear, pain, suffering, and disappointment. This theme in class got me thinking: the sooner they can learn those lessons, the sooner they can learn the truth about joy, courage, love, lightness—all those things we yearn for as adults.

If you are open to it, life has the natural ability to move you effortlessly to your next stage. It requires gratitude in the moment you currently find your-

self, in order to move into the next one.

It may feel like tightness in your heart, which could equate to you withholding love for some reason or another. Maybe there is old sadness that needs to be released, or forgiveness that needs to be granted. When you look into the darkness of your heart, I promise you there is a bright light shining just beyond the darkness, waiting to offer unconditional love to the world.

Take courage as another example. Ask yourself: What am I afraid of? Maybe it's something as simple as flipping over into a backbend. Are you afraid of what you can't see or where you are going? Are you afraid you will fall over?

Now take that same philosophy to something off your mat that you are afraid of. Maybe it's standing up for yourself. Move right into that fear and spell out all the things that would happen if you faced it. Then you can eliminate that fear and move forward! Fear immobilizes us from moving beyond ourselves. Find courage instead.

Starting today, I encourage you to begin noticing when you are suffering or when you are in pain. What are your most uncomfortable situations? How do you handle them? Do you avoid them? Distract yourself from them? The best thing you can do is to move into that pain fully. Jump right into it! Ask yourself: Why am I suffering? Try to pinpoint where that pain is coming from.

I promise you, if you begin noticing and then moving into it, beyond that pain and suffering is joy—pure joy.

Laughter

Have you ever caught yourself laughing so hard your sides felt like they were going to split open, or your cheeks hurt from laughing so hard? When was the last time you did that? Think back…when was it? Experts say we should laugh every day, that laughing actually boosts our immune systems and keeps

us healthy. How many of you laugh every day? Do you remember the last time you laughed?

Fortunately, my kids remind me to laugh pretty much every day. Somehow, it comes naturally to them—they see the humor in life, I guess.

It makes me wonder how we miss that in our day-to-day lives as adults. Laughter is at the seat of enlightenment. When you laugh, you are in the present moment— without judgment, fear, doubt, or any type of egoic thought. You are just expressing joy! You find this place where time stands still and you aren't caught up in what people are thinking, what you should be doing, or any type of unrealistic rationalization. You just ARE.

Laughter is the nectar that flows directly from the soul. When you laugh, you wake up your inner spirit and your internal guidance system; you touch your inner brightness and you are shining your light into the world.

When you laugh, you are one with the moment. For a nanosecond, you are liberated from your thinking mind and in alignment with your super-aliveness. You go back, even if only for a second, to who you were before conformity began. When your laughter is absolutely genuine, you can hear the whisper of your inner spirit assuring you that you may recapture your joy.

"Humor is the beginning of wisdom, and wisdom introduces us to Reality." What a profound statement. Much gratitude to Rev. Michael Beckwith for his words of wisdom and love.

Laugh today, at anything—laugh for REAL. Notice how it makes you feel: alive. Have a great day!

Giving and Receiving
In the Flow

I had an interesting conversation with my friends one evening about the idea around truly giving and then allowing others to give to us. We discussed the energy around this act of giving and receiving. It made me contemplate my own habits in this regard.

Let's say, for example, you give someone a compliment. You tell the person how great he or she looks. And instead of responding with a simple "Thank you," the person says "Oh, no I don't! I still have 10 pounds to lose! I have a long way to go." How does that make you feel as the giver of the compliment, having to spend energy on justifying how great he or she really looks? "Oh, yes you do! LOOK at you! You look fabulous!"

Does this sound familiar?

The energy involved in this communication is time consuming. The natural "flow" of the compliment is lost in judgments, justifications, validation, and small talk. Based on the person's response, will you readily give him or her a compliment again? Maybe, but maybe you won't because your last compliment turned into an energy-draining conversation.

Now let's apply that to other things we do. Say someone gives you homemade brownies in a Tupperware™ container. You are grateful but then give the container back to them filled with something else. Ha—have you ever done that? It's the "right" thing to do, right? Or is it?

Think about the spirit of receiving here for just one moment. You've been educated in the spirit of giving. But has anyone taught you about the spirit of receiving—how to receive something gratefully, knowing that it was meant to be, that you deserve it, that it's ok to just say, "Thank you?" Do you know how to allow that flow to come right up to you and to simply receive it?

I think I hear gasps. How can you do that—just take something without giving back? That's so selfish! What about even-Steven, tit for tat? What about keeping it fair?

The thing is, the Universe decides what is "fair," not you. You are here to just give and receive as it happens. You don't need to plan it, make sure it happens, or spend energy on creating "evenness" so you can feel good about giving or receiving something. It just happens.

I invite you now to do something for someone without letting him or her know it's you. Maybe pay for the car behind you in the coffee line, drop off some homemade jam at your neighbor's house, or something like that.

Now, even more difficult, when people give to you or do something nice for you, stop your thoughts in their tracks. Release the need to figure out how you can "pay them back." Just take it. Say "Thank you" and be done. Watch as your life unfolds with amazing gifts of joy and love and, dare I say, abundance.

Surrender

Surrender is an interesting word. To some, it means giving up—raising the proverbial white flag. It could also signify losing control or letting someone else win.

When I looked up "surrender" in the dictionary, one definition said, "To give oneself up into the power of another especially as a prisoner."

With this definition, in order to surrender, I have to relinquish control. But that does not have to be the truth of surrender. The truth is we don't have control, so how can we surrender or relinquish our control?

Holding on to the illusion of control only makes life tougher for you. You think you know what is best so you map out your life and try to push

circumstances in that direction. When you do this, you go against your Higher Power; you create unrest and turmoil within yourself. But if you surrendered, you would realize your Higher Power wants more for you than you can even conceive or imagine.

Surrendering means yielding to the power of another, but what if I suggested that the power of another is really yourself—that, in truth, you are a prisoner only to yourself and your beliefs, thoughts, and patterns? Hmmm, now this gets interesting.

You are continually evolving into new versions of yourself. The problem with the evolution of your soul is that, as a human being, you are hell bent on patterns— patterns of thought, behavior, responses, and the need to seemingly control your experiences. But what if you surrendered to your heart and those little voices that are trying to guide you?

That involves letting go, and if you let go your path might not be the one you thought it was going to be. You might be poor or single or live a life of perceived inadequacy. You might have to lose your job, divorce your spouse or move across the country.

But that's not the case—ever. When you let go and surrender to the gifts already inherent within yourself, your life shines brightly. You radiate love and abundance. But because the undertone of surrender is one of "giving up," you become fearful. What if you have to give up what you have? Then what? It's fear of the unknown.

Surrender means yielding to the power and gifts inherent within yourself. It means letting go of patterns inhibiting you from living your life full out. It means believing in the abundance and love that are there for you all the time.

That sounds so much better, doesn't it? Surrender—it's a natural progression and necessary in order to become your most authentic self.

Evolution

I don't know why, but I am always amazed by the Law of Attraction and how it works every single time without fail. Applying the Law of Attraction to self-growth and personal evolution is pretty much required if we are to recognize our most authentic selves.

For example, say you are experiencing a spiritual awakening and beginning to excavate your most authentic self. Along the way, you recognize a virtue (or two) that you would like to work on. Say you choose patience, compassion, or truth.

You may pray, meditate, or ask the Heavens, the Universe, or God to help you along this path. You may say, "Please, give me the opportunities to grow in this area of my Being." So you say it, and so it shall be. The question is, are you truly ready?

Because the truth is, once you ask, you shall receive— every single time. So here comes this opportunity that challenges your patience, compassion, or truth, and let's say you don't notice it as an opportunity. You fall into old patterns of behavior and thinking when faced with this particular opportunity. You respond in ways that feel comfortable to you but afterward, you feel uncomfortable. You realize later, Ah—that was an opportunity. Shoot, I did it again. I wish I had more patience; why didn't I show more compassion; why couldn't I tell the truth?

So you rationalize that next time you will get it right.

And the next time comes and again, you "fall short" of your own expectations. Maybe you even beat yourself up a bit. Oh man, again! Why did I do that again? I really don't want to act that way! That must be the conditioning

from my parents. I must have learned that from someone at work/school. You wallow in this agonizing self-pity only to miss the next opportunity to grow.

So what happens? Maybe you give up. You simply fall back into your old patterns—why? It's easier than growth. It's easier than getting back into the ring of Self Evolution which happens all the time with self-inquiry.

Understand that each and every time you ask to evolve, to grow, or to awaken, the heavens respond with circumstances that challenge you to do just that. And believe me, they aren't always fun circumstances.

> As Marianne Williamson said, "We must face our own ugliness. We often must become painfully aware of the unworkability of a pattern before we're willing to give it up. It often seems, in fact, that our lives get worse rather than better when we begin to work deeply on ourselves. Life doesn't actually get worse; it's just that we feel our own transgressions more because we're no longer anesthetized by unconsciousness."

What a powerful statement. We are *no longer anesthetized by unconsciousness.* We are awake and we see. In every moment, we see. So get in the ring of Self Evolution and keep asking for those opportunities. Become gratefully aware of your own self-growth and love hanging out with yourself, especially when you are not your best. That's when you need yourself the most.

Commitment and Dedication

What is it about summer that throws us so totally off course that we can't wait to get kids back to school again so we can go back to our schedules? Why can't we keep our schedules during the summer months? I admit that sometimes it's logistics, but honestly, what is it? If we were really committed to whatever it was we were "getting back to," why did we let it go in the first

place? Or why didn't we make the effort to keep it up no matter what got in the way?

Take yoga, for example. I know personally, I do not practice as much as I would like to over the summer when my kids are home. I have chosen on occasion to use the excuse, "Being at home with my kids is my yoga practice," which sounds so prophetic, doesn't it? But this simple observation made me question: Why didn't I commit to my asana practice? When were the moments that I chose something else instead of yoga? And why did I do that when I know how good yoga makes me feel?

Commitment, by definition, is "The state of being bound emotionally or intellectually to a course of action or to another person or persons." Commitment is a big word. What are we committed to? Our spouse or partner is an obvious answer. Our job...obvious. Other examples include completing projects or finishing our college degrees, training, or certification programs.

If commitment is such a strong word, I wonder why we sometimes use it so loosely.

Have you ever walked away from a relationship that you committed to? What about a job? How many times have you started a project and decided it was too much to keep up with so you gave up? What about good old New Year's resolutions—losing weight, quitting smoking, living healthier, talking nicer, exercising more? All these things are commitments, and sometimes we are excited to get going along a new path only to find that it is challenging to maintain. But *that* is where the learning takes place!

It's in that pivotal moment when you know you can either stray from your commitment or ask yourself: What is preventing me from keeping this commitment? What am I afraid of in this situation? Who could I become if I stuck with this?

Ask yourself: what are you committed to? Make a list. Pick just one thing you feel committed to—maybe it's a yoga class! Then do it! Put that one thing first! NOTICE when you start to make excuses or put other things first, and without beating yourself up, without judging, just ask yourself: Why? And then keep moving toward your commitment.

Commitments are steadfast and strong and should not be taken lightly. Make them good ones and keep it up!

Dimensions of Our Selves

As we move through this thing called life we are given labels based on what role we are playing at any particular moment. At any given time, we may be students, babysitters, committee members, sorority leaders, receptionists, assistants, college students, servers, triathletes, retail sales clerks, wives, managers, coaches, mothers, fathers, authors, PTA chairs, bus drivers, entrepreneurs, or retired executives.

You get the picture, right? There are so many things we CALL ourselves.

These are all just dimensions of our selves (our smaller selves, that is). Some of these labels will stay with us, but some will abruptly end. When they do, we must let them go. Why do we cling to them when they end—when we lose a job or end a relationship? Do we cling to them out of fear? Maybe we are afraid of what is yet to come. We ask, "Who am I if I am not a…" whatever the label is at that time.

What if we could let go of those labels that no longer define us? What if we could recognize those that will be around a good long time but still not be completely defined by them? Who we really are really isn't any of those labels. We may lose the label of an entrepreneur but we will always be a mother or father. See the difference?

But then who are we, really? Big question, isn't it?

HOW DO WE KNOW? I will tell you. We become still and ask to be awakened to the deepest dimension of our souls, the most real part of our Selves (our larger Selves, that is). We ask to be awakened to beauty, peace, love, joy, compassion, and forgiveness…we ask to live from there.

As you ask, so it shall be. And then those roles, those labels, float in and out of your life effortlessly. You are able to be a parent without losing your Self.

You are able to let go of labels that no longer define who you are. You are able to open up to the next stage of your evolution without resistance or fear, because you know who you are.

Ask yourself today: Who am I, really? What part of me is just a superficial, temporary dimension? What part of me is a lasting dimension? What part of me is real and deep and true?

Live from there—it's whole and true.

Detachment

Attachment is a really big challenge for most, and it's the root of all suffering. But how do you detach yourself from your material items, your titles, your community, your family, your children, and your identity? What does that mean, to detach yourself? Then what happens? This thought alone creates discomfort in the most peaceful of yogis.

And why? Patañjali says that this alone, *vairagyam*, or non-attachment, is the key to inner peace: "*The consciousness of self-mastery in one who is free from craving objects seen or heard about is non-attachment*" (Sutras 1:15).

Is this why so many people are unhappy, unfulfilled, disillusioned, and ill—because they go through life wanting and desiring things? Then how do you stop your attachment to these illusions of your life?

Here's more that can make non-attachment even more elusive:

The Vedantic scriptures say that "*Even the desire for liberation is a bondage.*" Sri Swami Satchisananda goes on to say that "*as long as the mind is there, its duty is to desire*" (Sutras 1:16).

So who is desiring—the Self, or the ego?

Wow—so now what?

Apparently, the key to inner peace is to desire without any personal or selfish motive—to have no expectation in anything we say, feel or do. In this way, we have no attachment to the outcome because we expect nothing.

When I hear this, karma yoga and selfless service come to mind. Losing everything comes to mind. When we have nothing, we have nothing to lose. This doesn't mean we can't own beautiful things, enjoy our families, or strive to get that promotion. It just means that we can detach ourselves from the outcome. We can enjoy that moment but be okay with it when it's over or if it never happens.

Still a difficult concept to digest? Most people get stuck when you begin discussing detachment from their families; in particular their children. As a parent, even thinking about this creates a lump in my throat. How can parents experience nonattachment to their kids? Aren't they supposed to be with them, guiding them, watching over them, teaching them, cuddling them, and disciplining them? How can parents possibly be detached from those little spirits that obviously NEED parental guidance?

Patañjali says to just enjoy being together, and that is all—to have no expectation. Someone else told me once that our goal as parents is to be able to let go accordingly—that it's a continuous process of letting go. This felt like a stab in my heart at first. My instinct is to protect my children, but what good does that do? Not much for them, and it's pretty selfish on my part.

However, having detachment from who our children are becoming and releasing expectation about who our children are right now creates a sense of lightness in even the most clinging of parents' hearts and minds.

Does it mean you can't fully love in order to detach? Absolutely not! It just means loving without attachment. It means allowing your heart to feel love and experience love without attachment to what may/may not be next. It's being in that moment of Divine connection.

The Isha Upanishad says, "Keep the heart in God and the head in the world. If you know how to put your heart in God, you can rest there always and still play in the world." I love that.

In the same way, we need never be afraid of the world if we learn to enjoy it without expectation—if we can detach ourselves and find only enjoyment in each moment.

Practice that this week. Enjoy what you have; enjoy each moment without expectation or attachment to it. See how light that feels.

Perfectly Imperfect

I was reading a book to my daughters the other night called Princess Perfect. I have no idea where this book came from but I read it anyway. This little Princess does everything perfectly—her room is clean and tidy, she brushes her hair without being asked, makes her bed, does her homework, eats all her vegetables, and goes to bed early without an argument.

Call me crazy, but that seems a little unrealistic. So my girls and I had a discussion about being perfect. I thought it was important because I can remember wanting to do everything perfectly. Why? I'm not sure. Maybe I was afraid of looking stupid. Maybe I thought I was supposed to know everything. Maybe I wanted approval from my parents, recognition from my peers, praise, celebrity, and notoriety—everything that had to do with my ego.

In times like this, when you have the insight to RECOGNIZE the ego, it's important to begin QUESTIONING your ego. To ask yourself: What am I REALLY afraid of if I don't appear to be perfect? What will happen if I don't know the answer? What will happen if I have to admit an ending of a relationship, a business, or a change of paths altogether? Oh my, what then? What's going to happen if people see that.your life isn't as perfect as you portray it to be? Will the sky fall?

Let's throw some questions out there for fun. To do everything "perfectly" means you are always right, right? That everyone else is "wrong." But who says what is right? Isn't it the goal of the ego to be right all the time? Who's

keeping track of what is right or wrong, anyway? Being perfect sure seems like a lot of responsibility to carry, if you ask me. Who wants to be right all the time? How tiring! And anyway, how CAN we be right all the time? Aren't we learning new things every day that may prove past theories to be outdated? Not wrong, just outdated.

Not only that, but why do you push yourself way out of your comfort zone, past your voice of reason, just to prove you are perfect? To prove that you have it "all figured out"? I'm not saying that you shouldn't do your best. What I am saying is that you can do your best without comparing yourself to others, without attaching an expectation to whatever it is that it will be without flaws or mistakes, and without killing yourself or sacrificing your soul's purpose just to prove you are perfect.

Why do you put up a front that everything is "perfect" when maybe it's not? Why are you afraid of saying, "Things aren't perfect and I need help," or "I don't know that answer—can you help me?" Why do you let your ego get so far ahead of you that finally, one day, you raise the white flag and say, "OK! I'm not perfect!" When this happens, you may feel like a failure or a disappointment.

Why do that when instead you could stop, breathe, and notice the aliveness in each moment? Can you even imagine what gifts would potentially come your way if you opened up to asking for help and then received it? You could stop fighting life in order to be perfect and instead allow life to happen around you. This opens you up to a state of spiritual instinct—your senses tell you that everything is going to be all right, even if you don't pass that test, perform that piece without mistakes, or keep your business going regardless of the circumstances.

You might spend so much of your life being what you think you are supposed to be, or a definition of what you think perfect is, that you may lose your Self along the way. But after a time, you will recognize that you are already perfect without being perfect. You are perfectly imperfect when you trust who you really are—the genuine Self that can withstand anything.

Sometimes it takes a loss to admit that perfection isn't all it's cracked up to be. You may lose your business, your home, your car, or your "friends," and you realize you are left with only your Self. But instead of being judgmental and self-loathing, you are full of strength and you realize that, really, you are exactly where you are meant to be— that change is the one thing you can rely on and that perfection is really only a state of someone else's mind.

Grace and Gratitude

Caroline Myss, author of Defy Gravity, defines "gravity" as something grave or serious. Therefore when we defy gravity, we are actually defying what is grave within ourselves.

Pretty insightful, if you ask me.

Something she said really resonated with me—hit me like a ton of bricks, actually. Let's see if I can recreate the experience for you. Ask yourself, right now: What do I deserve? What is rightfully mine? What am I entitled to? What have I worked so hard to attain? What is my reward? Before reading on, notice what your mind is telling you. What seems real for you right now when posed those questions? Are you entitled to a promotion, a beautiful home, an attentive spouse, unlimited financial resources, and perfect health?

Nope. Sorry…the answer is that you are entitled to nothing. That's right—nothing.

Did that shock you as much as it did me? At first I thought, Wow, you mean I'm not even entitled to breathe? Her response was no, you are not even entitled to breathe. Breathing in after an exhale is a gift, too. And until you have reverence for even the smallest thing like your breath, you are considered ungrateful.

In a split second, I got it. Of course I am not entitled to anything, and neither are you. Everything is a gift. That's right, a gift. Looking at life in this manner will open your eyes and heart to the magical moments that happen to you every day. It will help you to live in gratitude for all that you do have. It will wake you up to the inevitable fact that this day will never come again, and this moment is a once-in-a-lifetime moment.

If you can raise your awareness to this single statement, you will live in gratitude all the time. Wow. Look around you. What do you see now?

I'm not saying that we are meant to drop down to our knees in every moment and say, "Thank you!" The truth is, we are spiritual beings living a human experience and in order to connect to that powerful source of love, Divine energy, and connection of Oneness with all that Is, we must have reverence and gratitude. We must fall into the grace of gratitude as often as we can.

What does the grace of gratitude look like? Giving thanks for the obvious gifts in your life; that's easy. It's also giving thanks for the challenges that cross your path. They are gifts. In fact, those are the real gifts. They open you up to more than you thought possible. Let go of the perceived control you think you have and fall into your life. Let it carry you along with intention and purpose.

When you give thanks for that Divine power of love and equanimity, you truly can defy gravity, every single time.

Carrying Our Stuff

Everyone carries around "stuff" with them. Everyone has something they are grieving about, working on, deciding upon, contemplating, challenging themselves with—everyone has "stuff." This type of turmoil is a normal part of the human experience—in fact, it's kind of a prerequisite. This is what you signed on for when you agreed to incarnate into this life: "stuff."

Can you imagine a life without turmoil, questions, and decisions? Where would the growth happen? How would you ever remember your inner radiance without your inner turmoil?

The downside is that all this turmoil creates dis-ease in the body. Somewhere, you harbor dis-ease in your physical body. It is normal, so it's ok to experience disease, but energetically speaking, the goal is to get that dis-ease to

move—to flow through the physical body without stagnating or getting stuck anywhere in the subtle body.

As human beings, though, we don't let it flow—we hold onto it. We suffer over and over again. We replay memories in our minds that cause us pain without moving past it. We are gripped with fear when we have to make decisions...what if we make the wrong one? We continue to beat ourselves up for something we did years ago that has nothing to do with who we are now. We cover it all up and busy ourselves with things that mean nothing to us. We pack our schedules so tight that we have no time to go inward and face what is causing the dis-ease. We allow it to continue to embed itself in our bodies physically, emotionally, and spiritually.

So now what? The answer is simple. To be free from dis-ease, change the weight of the seriousness about the circumstance or blockage, and in doing so you change the wait of your healing and move beyond your circumstance.

Think about that for a minute. Change the weight of the seriousness about the circumstance. How much does this event weigh on you, your thoughts, and your decisions? Why? What belief keeps you rooted in that event, making you replay it over and over again until you "figure it out"? I'll bet that when you get to the root of the issue, even the weight you place on that event or circumstance is totally out of your control.

When you let go and stop allowing life to kick you and drop you to your knees, you can be free from dis-ease in the body and move forward to the life you were meant to experience. You can continue along your path of spiritual awareness, growth, and development without looking back at events that control you and drop you into stagnation.

Change the weight of the seriousness...let it go. Laugh about it. Fall into it. Be free from it. Let energy flow to and from you effortlessly.

Sense of Urgency

Does anyone else feel a sense of urgency to serve the world? Do you feel this wave of change happening as you sit at your desk? You just KNOW things are changing but you have no idea what to do or where to start? You just KNOW that times are changing and you can either change along with them consciously or continue along your path of a robotic existence?

But how can you possibly make change or serve someone else or a higher purpose? There are bills to pay, jobs to keep, kids to raise…so many things to "do" in your "cube of life."

Sorry to tell you this, but when you feel this sense of urgency, it means it is time for you to prepare.

Prepare for what? Empowerment, enlightenment, conscious aliveness, divine wholeness…call it what you like; it's awakening!

Are you ready for that? I think of Arjuna from the Bhagavad Gita, ready to put down his sword when he realized he was fighting his family, ready to give up out of fear. But really, what was he fighting? Himself and his own beliefs. What makes us different from Arjuna? Nothing.

The reality is that some of us like the complacency offered by routine and expectancy. But that is not to be. Life is impermanent—it's ever changing and always flowing from one stage to the next. And right now, like it or not, it is time to wake up and live life consciously.

What if I told you that the images you see and choose to focus on become your reality? That you actually DO have a say in what you see and experience every single day of your life? Would you believe me, or would you like to believe that you are just a victim, watching a movie that is pre-destined to be your life?

Let me awaken you for a moment: You have the power to create your reality. Yes, amidst all the Hollywood blockbusters, news media, and reality programs, YOU have the power to choose what you want to see.

This is where life gets good. The time is NOW to understand the importance of disciplining your thoughts so your reality truly reflects your inner perception. Along this quest for wholeness and reality, what are we all up against, really?

The media. Hollywood. Politicians. Other people's ideas and perceptions of what reality truly is.

Pretty daunting battle, I have to admit—if you are asleep. But if you are awake, it's no problem. You can do it. You can choose. Ask yourself: What do I want right now—for me, for my children, for my future? Do I want competition or cooperation with others? Fear or love for others? Oneness with others, or separateness that divides? Which is it? Because this is important.

Patañjali said thousands of years ago that the key to life is disciplining your thoughts. And here you are, inundated with so much media that you are confused about what is reality and what is illusion. The time is now to discipline your thoughts and discern what is truth and what is illusion.

The time is now to stop, practice yoga, meditate, pray, affirm—get close to that inner YOU and decide where you want your life to be.

I choose love. I choose cooperation. I choose Oneness. Are you with me?

The Path of Yoga

What is the path of a yogi, anyway? What is yoga? Is there one path or lineage that is better than another, a style that is more comprehensive than another? What is the "goal"?

The answer is no—no *one* style is better than another. Every style or path leads to the same thing: spiritual awakening and liberation, a release of bondage to the ego, freedom from negative patterns, and empowerment. The physical postures of yoga are not only designed to provide you with flexibility and strength but are also the greatest tool in creating stillness of the mind and harmony between mind, body, and spirit.

BKS Iyengar says that most people come to yoga—the physical practice of yoga, that is—for physical reasons: a bad back, a sports injury, or high blood pressure. Most often, it has to do with something involved with one's lifestyle, weight, level of stress, or addictions.

What is so interesting, though, is that the goal of yoga is ultimate freedom from anxiety, more self-control, and self-awareness so you can live the life you were meant to live. How do you do that? By dropping the ego. How do you do that? By recognizing you are separate from the ego. How do you do that? By concentrating inwardly in an otherwise hectic world.

And according to BKS Iyengar—thank you for confirming this, my old friend— this is accomplished through the practice of relaxing the brain through yoga postures!

For each of you out there considering yoga: do it! Your physical body is a direct manifestation of your spiritual being. When you begin the journey of

aligning the body physically, detoxifying your impurities, and following your heart in everything you do, you become your Self— with a capital S.

Just start it for physical reasons and see what happens. See how your body changes, and then see if the changes flow over into the remaining areas of your life. You will be glad you did!

Say Yes!

Just five weeks prior to my first mission trip to the Dominican Republic, I woke up in a panic. I found myself with so many mixed emotions. I was going to be gone, away from family, phones, and internet for 10 days. All my work stuff would have to wait. There was a fun carnival at my daughters' school that week that I would miss. I was riddled with fear, guilt and worry.

Immediately, I began thinking about ways I could get out of this trip. Why? Why did I want out? Fear. Loss of control. I had to ask myself: What was I afraid of? Was I really in control of anything as it was anyway? Interesting, isn't it?

I began to work myself up about what would go on while I was away. How could anyone possibly take care of the kids while I was gone? Oh, my— what will my house look like? Who's going to remember to feed the cats and the fish? Will the girls brush their hair and teeth every day? Is their homework going to get done? What about dance, gymnastics, and theater?

Tired yet?

Exactly. Up until that moment, I had assumed responsibility for all of those things. No wonder I was panicked. That's a ton of control! I had to let go. I know this resonates with some of you because I've witnessed you not giving yourselves permission to go away even overnight by yourself, justifying this by saying, "I have to be at home. Who will take care of everything?"

I also see some of you stay in jobs you hate just so you can pay your bills, putting off what you really love to do for another time in your life. Why—because you have "things" to do, because you have responsibilities that take precedence?

Guess what—when you think like that, like you have to control life and put things off because of your responsibilities, you become resentful and you lack a zest for what life is really about. You stay comfortable in your shell and complacent in your actions. Not only that, but if you do have children, what message does it send to them? To postpone their own dreams for a perfect time?

I'm not telling you to run off to an impoverished country and be a "do-gooder." I am only suggesting that you look at your life and notice if you are holding back. Are you underestimating the power you have within because of fears and negative thinking? Are you saying "no" to opportunities because you fear a loss of control?

If you are, notice it and be aware. Ask yourself: What are my top five or even 10 passions? Am I doing any of those things? Why am I not doing these things? What am I afraid of? Is it a valid fear? Most likely, it isn't.

Make this a year that is full of vibrant energy! Say YES!

Concentration

In yoga, we learn how to discipline the mind—not to control the mind, but to discipline the mind. Why would you want to do such a thing?

Because if you are to live a life that is truly yours then your mind must be disciplined. If you are to fulfill your purpose or destiny in life, a commitment to discipline of the mind is essential. Some of you may be thinking, I already control my mind. No one tells me what to think! But I am here to tell you that you are incorrect.

As long as you are a human being, you are distracted by outside influences in one way or another, and the only way to overcome that is to discipline your mind.

Where to start? You guessed it—a dedicated yoga practice. Staying focused on your breath while holding a yoga posture for even just a moment is quite a challenge for Westerners! Our minds jump around like monkeys, thinking about what we need to do, how we look, or even what we forgot to do or say earlier. Discipline of the mind involves several concepts, but it simply starts with the physical practice of yoga.

Hatha yoga poses were actually designed just for that reason: to discipline the mind so we can become laser sharp in our focus and extremely intentional in our actions.

Why would you want a laser sharp focus in life? So you can concentrate on one thing at a time. Why would you want to do that? Because being distracted thinking about many things at one time creates stress in the body and eventually dis-ease.

See where this is going? Physically practicing yoga brings better health!

But what does it mean to concentrate? It means you have an aim in life—a purpose or goal. You wake up with intention and deliberation. It means you are not swayed by what other people think. You choose what to think regardless of outside distractions.

But how many times do you allow others to shift your focus of what you think is important? Honestly, how often do you change course based upon other people's perceptions?

Concentration is essential for a strong mind. As a society, we have lost our power to concentrate because of all the distractions in our peripheral vision. We have technological advances that keep us "on top" of everything but also keep us from focusing on one thing at a time. Not only that, but we have so many choices that we can't possibly focus on one thing—we think, we MUST be missing out on something better!

Concentration breeds commitment. When you stay focused you are committed. Isn't that interesting to think about? Think about failed relationships, lost jobs, or unfinished programs…you lacked commitment, but really you lacked concentration. You got distracted.

94

Ask yourself: How often have I lost my focus? Be kind to yourself and lose the judgment—it's normal! Do you want to make a change? If you do, try this:

> Wake up every morning and just sit for 10 rounds of deep breathing. Sounds easy, right? Good—that way you will try it. Sit up in your bed and just breathe. Focus only on the breath traveling in and out of your nose. Now notice how many thoughts come into your mind. Let them go by allowing them to float by—just notice is all. If you can practice this for one week, you will see a marked difference in your concentration and increased awareness in your life. These five minutes every morning will offer you so much more time.

You will be amazed and ask yourself why you didn't start this a long time ago!

Patience

In disciplining the mind, I think it is important to not only talk about concentration but also patience. Why? Because we are a society that is accustomed to having everything right NOW! Not in five minutes, not in a day, but right now! We are all about instant gratification— and it's only getting worse.

If you have kids, don't you find it difficult to tell them, "Just be patient," when they see you zipping on the computer or your phone to find directions to where you need to be? (Does anyone even use a phonebook anymore?)

Let's look at patience from an "on the mat" perspective. From a student's point of view, why would you want to cultivate patience? So you can get deeper into your physical postures, right? So you can find that block that is giving you trouble or holding you back from going beyond that discomfort to a more open variation of the pose.

What about from a teacher's standpoint? Why would teachers want to cultivate patience? Let me ask you this: Could you imagine attending a yoga class with a teacher who wasn't patient—who said to you, "Do you not hear what I am saying to you? Lift your leg higher"? Would you go back to class after that?

Now let's look at patience from an "off the mat" experience. There are so many examples and opportunities to practice patience, aren't there? How about this: try picking the longest line at the bank or the grocery store—I dare you. Talk about patience! What about watching your child tie his or her shoe in the morning when you are late for work already? What about noticing how you beat yourself up mentally when you revert to old habits of behavior even when you know they don't serve you anymore and you really want to make a change but don't know how?

Do you have patience for yourself?

That's the place to start…with you. But how? You guessed it—starting physically, "on the mat," in yoga with Savasana—Final Relaxation. Again, I dare you. I still remember the first yoga class I went to. The teacher told us at the end of class to lie there, completely still, and breathe. And I thought, Why? I have to go! I have to…do *something*. That's the paradigm—we think we have to do something when really what we NEED to do is be still and cultivate patience. Do you really NOT have five minutes to be still? Not even five minutes—*really*?

We live in a society where everything—I mean everything— is at our fingertips. NOW is the most important time to cultivate patience. Why get to where you are going before it's time? Remember wanting to grow up really fast? Now look at you, you're there! Now what?

Mmm hmm….try Savasana; lie there on your back and just breathe. Close your eyes but be mindful—the mind will wander and you will think about all sorts of things. Better to focus on something on the ceiling. Just breathe in and out. Don't move a muscle; don't get water; don't think about how you have to use the restroom. Just lay there in stillness—set a timer if you have to. Only five minutes. Try it and see how patient you become.

Faith

I was raised Catholic and was taught that the only faith that meant anything was God in Heaven. Anything beyond that, any other religion or thought, was wrong. No need to even research it.

My children go to Catholic school now, so on some level, I resonate with principles from this religion—even if I walked away from it for quite a while. I have come back to it now with a whole new perspective because of all the various books, religions, and faith-based communities I have been exposed to over the years—and thankfully so, because now the word "faith" means so much more.

I have, however, come to a simple definition of faith that I think everyone can relate to. Beyond all religions, there is one thing that faith can encompass and embody: faith in yourself.

How can that be? What about God? Or Buddha? Or another Deity we can find faith in—any other "god" that can fix things for us, make things happen, answer our prayers? Sounds cliché however, the only power that truly exists is the power within.

Faith begins internally so looking outside yourself will never work. Deep down, we are made in the image and likeness of God. We are Godlike, so if we have faith in ourselves then we have faith in our Higher Power of belief.

Why is faith important? Because it makes you steadfast and strong. Because you then recognize the power you have within you to make your life your own. You ask for guidance, yes…always ask for guidance… USE that faith in YOUR Higher Power! But realize that you are truly asking your heart of hearts for that guidance, not a guy with white billowy robes and a long gray beard. You are asking your SELF, which is a physical manifestation of your own soul made in the likeness of God.

Ask yourself: When do I lack faith in myself? You lack faith whenever you think or do something that does not serve your inner light: when you smoke, take drugs, or continually eat food that is unhealthy for you; when you lack faith in your abilities and shortchange yourself from experiencing a life that you dream of and instead settle for what you think is the "right" thing to do. Whenever you harm your physical body in any way that keeps you from realizing your Divine nature, you lack faith.

You are basically saying, "I can't do it. I can't be all that I can be so I will settle for this." Sounds silly, yes, but it's true. There is nothing that can make you be less than you are meant to be but your own mind. And it's only your mind that lacks faith when this happens—your heart is open, but your mind takes over.

God has a plan for each of us—we choose to incarnate with a plan….a purpose. Each of us is called to that purpose time and time again. Why don't you live up to His calling? What are you afraid of? I will tell you why… because you are afraid of being all that you can be—what a high standard to live up to! When you are all that you can be, well, then you may fall short. This is where you lack faith.

If you can recognize the beauty of life, the Divinity of "coincidence," and the power within yourself, you can truly live a life full of faith. You can go out and be, do, and contribute to this life because you know, beyond all knowing, that you will be taken care of—that the Universe, God, or Source is working to deliver you to your Highest Self in every moment.

How do you cultivate faith? Start with yoga. It's that stillness that makes yoga so different from any other practice. If you go back to the purpose for Hatha Yoga postures—*to use the physical body to bring the spiritual body toward consciousness*—it makes complete sense. You walk into yoga class thinking, "There is no way I can touch my toes or bring my head to my knee!" And within a week or two, you are doing it—you have physically disciplined the mind in order to perform a pose. You now have faith in yourself.

Now you can go out and have more self-esteem. You can quit doing drugs, eating horribly, smoking, yelling, acting out—whatever your "addiction" is, you simply stop because you know you can. Then your physical body becomes lighter and more able to hear the guidance all around you, all the time. That's faith.

Affirmations & Postures

Stop trying to change the world. Just make conscious choices for your Self and you will witness exponential shifts in the world you are currently watching.

Understand that every system of roots, pile of rocks, or other challenge in your path to simplicity is there for you to dig into. Get dirty and get to the bottom of it, so you can grow and fully bloom into your truest self in the "spot" you picked in the yard of your life.

When you stop leading others and just lead yourself, your life becomes a true manifestation of who really are and even better, who you are becoming.

The Now is good! It may feel or look different than what you thought it was going to be but we're not meant to judge it; we're only meant to live it.

Laugh today, at anything—laugh for REAL. Notice how it makes you feel: alive.

Bless and surrender the past, for in doing so, you will reclaim the joy in life.

Commitments are steadfast and strong and should not be taken lightly. Make them good ones and keep it up!

Boat

Gate

Plank

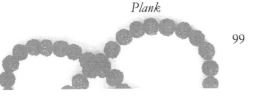

Sidebend

Triangle

Twist

Warrior I

Halfmoon

Reverse Warrior

Chapter 4
On Grief versus Love
Heart Chakra: Anahata

Self-Discipline

Why do we want to master the mind again? So we can quiet it down so the heart can sing. It's been said that the mind is like a bad neighborhood...stay away. However, it may be more advantageous to get in there and master it instead.

An important key to mastering the mind is self-control. Personally, for me, the word control creates tension, so instead, let's say harness or dare I suggest, self-discipline again. These two words can be illustrated in so many ways.

Bikram talks about self-control as distinguishing between a need and a want. Being able to have enough discipline of the mind to take a breath before following the egoic need toward a want. How many times are you choosing to follow a want when your basic needs are not truly met? And after satisfying that want, realizing that on a deeper level you are truly unsatisfied because your needs are not met. Following your wants without awareness is a vicious, never-ending cycle.

But how else can we define self-discipline or self-control? What about when you wake up to your Self and you recognize those moments that move you away from who you really are and keep you stuck in old habits, behaviors, and patterns? Scientifically, we are programmed beings—following a program in our brain so faithfully that we don't always question our actions—we just do.

But that day, when you wake up and begin to see the world consciously, life begins moving in slow motion so moment by moment, you can choose your thoughts and your reactions. You can use self-discipline to change the patterned thoughts of who you have been and instead become who you are meant to be.

How do you do that? Yes, through the practice of yoga. As always, I equate your yoga practice on the mat to your life practice off the mat.

First off, self-discipline just to get to a yoga class is huge. How many times have you heard yourself say, "I really need to do yoga," but do you? Maybe you do, maybe you don't. Once you get there and you encounter a pose that is too difficult or challenging, how do you handle it? Do you back off admitting, "I can't do that," or do you go beyond your abilities and find a deeper edge?

Do you come back to class time and time again to discipline your body or do you make excuses about why you can't get there or why you can't do a pose? How do you feel in a Hot Yoga class when the heat is stifling enough to choke you? Do you get up and leave or do you say to yourself, "I can do this." Regardless of how you answered those questions, it's very likely you answered exactly how you navigate through life off the mat, too.

Those are examples of disciplining the body through a yoga practice. But remember, our bodies and our yoga practice are just physical manifestations of our minds and hearts. Now switch gears for a moment and look at your life. How do you define self-discipline?

Take something simple like eating. Something you do every day; something that is necessary to sustain your life.. When you recognize that what you put into your mouth isn't just sustaining or nourishing you, in fact, it's creating density, what do you do? Do you eat it anyway or do you choose another option? You may justify a binge by saying, "I deserve this." Great! So do I, but not to the point of feeling bad about what I have eaten. Ask yourself, why do I love to eat? And how could I eat better so my physical body would feel better? Clear those energy lines for a truer awakening of the Self.

We can also look at our behavioral patterns. How do you react when you are hurt, upset, or angry? Do you lash out or do you take a moment to sit in your pain and explore why are you feeling that way? Finding self-discipline in those moments means sitting with your pain, even for a breath. Take the time to look inward and recognize that all pain is your own and no one is to blame.

Life is clearer when we find self-discipline. We begin to shed layers of density—physically, emotionally, and mentally. What we are left with is our true Self—our inner, bright being. Self-discipline helps us to decide moment by moment, what is best for our most spiritual, awakened being.

You Can Do Both

Prior to my firsty mission trip to the Dominican Republic, I was filled with doubt and continual questions about what I was preparing to embark upon. I was, at the time, living a traditional, predictable life, full of responsibility and obligation. Each day had a schedule that I upheld. Before I got married, secured a mortgage, and had children, I had lived a life of wanderlust, filling myself with consciousness by traveling to foreign countries and allowing experiences to carry me to the next part of my life. This type of life set my heart on fire like nothing I had ever experienced.

I always loved living like this, with no commitment, no worries, and no deadlines—just being in the moment. So after seven years of living a predictable, regimented, scheduled life, you can imagine how I felt when I was tossed into my "prior life" of wanderlust on my trip to the Dominican Republic.

You guessed it—great.

There was an undeniable sense of wholeness I felt being in the Dominican Republic. No technology, new people, and a deep, important, global purpose sparked my heart! I enjoyed living in the moment and being one with the community of Habanero. No pretenses, no expectations, no greed, and no underlying agendas. It felt so amazing.

Understanding that in order to come back to my predictable life gracefully, I had to compare the two lifestyles and recognize how they were so different, yet the same. I couldn't come back and not use the Internet, get upset when my kids didn't get along, give their toys and clothes away, and walk to work.

I also, quite honestly enjoy the fact that I can drink my water, take a hot shower, wash my hair every day, turn on my electricity, and use the restroom without any issues.

I had to wonder though, which lifestyle was better for my soul. Finally, after three days back, I realized both were important. But an unexpected truth that came out of that experience was that one cannot survive completely without the other. The polarity is necessary for the survival and growth of my soul.

Thankfully, because of the choices I have made in my life, I can have both. But how many times do we suffer because we allow ourselves to think we have to choose?

We play a movie in our head that says that our life can only be one way. We tell ourselves that we should just be happy with what we have, yet we continually wish for something different. We put off our heart's desire for later thinking that we cannot experience both lives at the same time. It's only years later after our kids are gone, that we are resentful and unhappy because we left a part of us unfulfilled. Buddha says these are the issues that cause all of our suffering.

You can have it all in this lifetime simultaneously, but only if you know beyond all knowing what it is that truly fills your soul. Allow yourself the freedom to dream; don't put anything off until tomorrow. Don't be afraid and don't wait. Life is waiting for you to grab it and live it fully and completely. Your heart will open up to life's gifts if you let go and be.

Expectation

During yoga classes, I constantly remind students to release expectations of themselves when they come to their mat. In a Vinyasa class, each class is different, like an organic dance with a theme to guide it, so releasing expectation is easy—you never know what is coming up next! Still, a subtle reminder is necessary to remind us to release expectation because we are so used to expecting so much from ourselves off our mat, why not on it, right?

Now in a Bikram Yoga class, it's a little more difficult to release expectation. The poses are exactly the same every class, you KNOW it's going to be stifling hot in the room, and the instructors all use the same dialogue.

Your mind has many opportunities to wander and take over. "Today I am going to lock that knee and balance!" And then what happens when you don't balance? Disappointment and suffering. Then the mind goes on autopilot: "Am I ever going to balance? Why can't I balance? What is wrong with me? Why can't I look like her/him? What the hell am I doing here?" One thought spirals to the next and all of a sudden, your practice is gone.

Let's relate expectation to any circumstance off the mat. Pick one—any one. Any circumstance that you held an expectation to the end result. Countless circumstances in your day-to-day life offer you the opportunity to ATTACH an expectation to the outcome.

Need examples? How about when you brought home flowers for your girlfriend? Or bought a new bike that you were excited about? Or you wore a new outfit? Got your hair done differently? Applied for a job? Told someone that you loved them? I could go on and on for days… you get the picture. Before reading on, call to mind one of your own life experiences that means something personal to you. If any of these situations left you feeling frustrated or disappointed… you were expecting something.

What would it look like if there was no expectation to your action? What if you just did things without expecting anything in return? What if you did things just for your own personal joy? What if you just did what you did and didn't expect anything from anyone? Or better yet, what if you lived life not expecting life to GIVE anything to you? You just lived… what would that look like?

Boundless—blissful—enjoyable—lovely….

Does that mean you have to be passive to the events that take place in your life? No. It just means that you can allow life to happen without attaching to what you think should or should not be in any given moment because of what you have thought, done, or said.

Your "nature" is to expect, but that's your EGO nature, not your BUDDHA nature. As a human, you are TAUGHT to expect… you don't come into this world expecting anything—you just are. Expecting is learned and defined for you by people who are important to you: parents, teachers, siblings, and friends.

Remind yourself today that you are a spiritual being living a human experience and that to expect is human, not spiritual. Expect nothing—you will never be disappointed.

Judgment

The evil twin to expectation is judgment. They go hand in hand and they spell trouble whenever they are together.

Remember that expectations are learned thoughts. We are TAUGHT to expect. Your ego expects love, respect, cooperation, understanding, fairness, compassion, empathy, honesty. And when you don't get those things, you suffer, right? When you don't get what you expect, you almost always judge the other person or the experience. You judge, with your limited perception, why and how such a thing could happen.

"If he loved me, he wouldn't go on that week-long golf trip." "That poor child must have a tough home life— it's difficult to get him to cooperate." "She must not care about what's going on in my life—she's not even looking at me when I'm talking to her."

Take a look at each of those statements. First, there is an expectation. I expect him to show me he loves me by staying home with me. I expect the child to cooperate and do things my way. I expect her to look at me when I am talking to her.

Remember how dangerous expectations are. They set up the perfect playground for judgments.

Can we really believe that someone doesn't love us because they want to go on a golf trip? Or that a child has a tough time at home because he doesn't cooperate in school? Or that someone doesn't care just because they aren't looking at us? No. These are all our personal judgments of the situation. And judgments are born from our perceptions from past experiences, from parental ideas about past experiences.

The trick is to notice—immediately—when you are judging a situation. This is challenging because judgments are trained thoughts that just happen automatically. Your mind goes on autopilot and judges everything and everyone. It's how it weeds out "good from bad."

So my challenge for you is to notice. Notice when you are judging a situation. Why is this helpful? Well, for several reasons. One is that not everyone wants to hear your judgment about a situation or a person. They want to make their own judgment and that's important because we all have different perceptions of the world.

Another reason is because most often, judgments are knee-jerk reactions that can hurt people. They are not usually thought out and scrutinized. Besides that, how can we EVER have enough information about anything to make a judgment?

And the most important reason to limit your judging is because if we are all made of energy, and energy can never be created or destroyed, where do you think that judgment ends up? Mmmhmm—right back at you!

Shine Your Little Light

So you're shining your little light, are you? Being your best? Everything is going just fabulous! Actually, it seems quite magical. People and situations are manifesting in your life just how you have envisioned them. It seems as if the Universe is truly supporting you every second. You know it, you feel it.

And then you spend some time with people who knew you before you began shining your little light. For example, you visit your family or old friends. You may even be in a situation where someone close to you, like your spouse or partner, really isn't "on board" with this new you that shines so brightly.

Without knowing it, you are put in the position of continuing to shine or dimming your little light just a bit so they can feel better around you. I mean after all, what would they think if all of a sudden you woke up and meditated every day, put yourself first, remained calm in stressful situations, stopped drinking alcohol, and ate only healthy food? Really—what the heck would they think?

People closest to you expect you to act and react in a certain way. What would happen if you were all of a sudden different? How would they react to you? I can tell you, they would be very confused and they would get very upset. They wouldn't know what to do. I mean, after all this habitual behavior; what do we do now?

If you keep in mind for a minute that about 90 percent of your 70,000 thoughts a day are patterned, it's easy to imagine the scenario when you take the road less traveled. Those are the mirrors of your old self, reflecting old experiences of resistance, guilt trips, and negative feedback just to see if you are for REAL. It's like someone who continues to poke you in the arm until you finally swat their hand and yell "Stop it already!" Then they can say, "See I knew you would finally crack. Ah, I feel much better now. This reaction is what I am used to."

When you are on the road to transformation—I mean REAL transformation—it's not always easy. In fact, if it were easy, everyone would do it. The truth is that it's easier to live in patterned thoughts and behaviors, blame others for your mediocre life, and surrender to the negative patterns you have adopted along your life path.

It's much harder to break patterns and change your karma. Because that's what you do when you shine your light; you change your karma. And some of the specimens in your life don't want you to change your karma. They want you to stay just how you are because... guess what? THEY are fearful of losing you... THEY are attached to the way it's always been... THEY are learning from you and they want you to stick around.

But it doesn't have to be. No, it can be just the way you envision it. And you don't have to lose the people closest to you. You just continue along your little path of love and light and keep on shining. That's all you have to do. They will get on board, watch from a distance, or bid you farewell. And that's not your choice; it's theirs.

I know it's scary. You think you will be alone on that journey. But you won't— I promise. You will be surrounded by people, places, and situations that support your soul intention. Your life will become magical. Trust the Universe; shine brightly and see what happens. It feels much better than the alternative.

Walking the Line

When you start on an inner journey or spiritual trek, the road can be bumpy. There are lots of detours, potholes, wrong turns, and dead ends. In fact, a lot of the time it's easier to go back or even give up. But the reality is that you can never give up on a spiritual trek—once you begin, that's it.

You have ignited a flame within you, illuminating the spiritual being that you really are, and now that's it's finally been noticed, no matter what you do, it will never go out. Recognizing this illumination can be addicting; especially if you live a chaotic or stressful life. Now that you have experienced that natural state of inner peace, why would you want to go back to anything else?

Meditating, yoga classes, hikes, silent walks through the trees or along the beach, yoga retreats… it all sounds like heaven. Going back to your "real" life after these types of experiences can look less than appealing once you begin this journey.

But I am here to tell you that there is no real difference between the two. The only reason you are suffering and creating aversion to your "real" life is because you perceive them to be different. It's always about perception. Trust me; I know they certainly don't SEEM the same… believe me… I KNOW! My life is nothing short of organized chaos on any given day at any given moment. Unless of course my kids are sleeping.

However, there are three things going on here that I would like you to be aware of:

1.   You are suffering because you feel that getting away will solve it all. That's an illusion. It's just a little easier to focus without distraction so the journey to the Self is much clearer.

2.   You grasp for what you think life could be like if you didn't have all those distractions. You imagine you would be more at peace without all the noise and negative energy.

3.　　　You perceive your "real" life to be hard and unfulfilling when in reality, you can change your perception about it all and experience santosha in even the most difficult moments.

It's easy for anyone to find inner peace on a retreat, in a yoga class, during a meditation session or while enjoying a vacation. But what if you could experience that same feeling in your "real" life? You can. It's just a matter of changing your perception.

How? Use different words to describe your real life. Recognize gratitude for every single thing in your real life. Express appreciation for all that you have. Breathe during stressful moments; it just takes 90 seconds for an emotion to pass.

Anyone can find peace in a cave. The ancient yogic texts weren't written by working executives, stay-at-home moms, or single parents. They were written by sages who went up into the mountain, renounced all personal possessions, and contemplated life.

Be grateful! You get to reap those benefits and you don't have to renounce anything!

Back-floating

For a while, I was teaching kids' yoga to the children at my daughters' school. It was such a blessing to share time with these kids. I learned so much from them every week. We did yoga, played games, discussed life virtues, and I usually had them each take a turn introducing a new pose to the class.

The children's ages ranged from two and a half to 11 years old and it always amazed me how awake, alive, and connected these children were. To be honest, adults could stand to learn a ton from them.

One day, this gorgeous little boy named Griffin got up and said, "My pose today is called back-floating." He then laid down on the mat in Svasana (Corpse

Pose) which is the traditional way to end any yoga class. My eyes filled with tears as I realized in that moment how incredible this really was.

Now, you may be thinking… "What's the big deal?", so let me shed some light on this.

First off, Svasana is the most important pose in yoga. It's performed at the end of the class so all the work you do during class can settle into the cells and literally rejuvenate the body. It's also the most difficult pose because if you move a muscle or think a thought you have lost the pose.

Griffin just plopped down and did it—eyes closed, arms at his sides, completely relaxed. And he waited there until everyone else did the pose with him. He didn't look around, he didn't move a muscle. He just trusted that everyone would follow his lead, and they did. I compare this to adults I witness having a hard time lying there for five minutes and can't help but marvel at how it just comes naturally to these kids.

Secondly, it made me really think about this pose as "backfloating" instead of Corpse Pose for a moment. In back-floating, we can imagine we are literally floating on our back near the shore of a lake or river. We are completely supported by the water—we have nothing to fear. We trust that the water will support us—there's no question about it. We don't ask why we float, or how we float, we just DO.

If we dig just a little deeper, we can imagine the entire Universe supporting us in this way. I mean, if a current of water that flows effortlessly, connected to the Earth can support us… of course, this is just representative of the Universe supporting us, right?

And then I began to think about how as humans we usually fight that current or Universal support. We tread water, we dog-paddle, we swim ferociously… we do everything but just float with no worries.

And then I thought about how this wonderful little spiritual being just woke me up again. He reminded me of the power in truly trusting the Universe. Somewhere along the way we were taught that we have to do all this really hard work to make things happen, but if we just simply back-floated, everything would turn out just fine!

And thanks Griffin… you always amaze me, dear one!

Acceptance

How many times have you fought what is real for you? By that I mean, how many times do you wish things were different?

Take any example: what job you have, where you live, the relationship you have with your parents, spouse or children, or what situation you are in at any point in time. How many times do you waste the time away wishing things were different? This is the root of suffering for almost all human beings… attachment to what we think things should be like.

He should love me this way, the kids should get along, I should have a great relationship with my brother/sister/mother/father, I should be at a certain stature in my career by now, I should live in a better neighborhood…

So let's make this colorful, shall we? Let's say you have a less than desirable relationship with your mother. In fact, whenever you spend time with her, you get stressed. You just have trouble being yourself.

Ask yourself why? Why are you feeling that way? I can tell you: because you have a perception of what that relationship is supposed to look like. Because you have an expectation and a judgment of what is "right" and "acceptable."

But who says it's supposed to be a certain way? What would happen if instead, you looked at that relationship for what it was and just—dare I say it?—accepted it as it was being presented to you? What doors would open then? How much freer would you feel?

Not only that, but if you could accept the relationship as it was, imagine how much more space you'd have for love and compassion?

I would like to dig just a tad deeper if I may.

What if you accepted the belief that we pick our parents? We pick our parents because we have something to teach them? We have things to learn, sure,

115

but on a more ethereal level we chose them to teach them something. Now how easy is it to recognize what gift needs to be birthed? Now can you feel compassion?

When we accept things as they are, we may suffer for a bit. But remember that when we suffer, it's just the mind having issues with what is. Once we move past that suffering and realize it's not serving our happiness to suffer any longer, then we move into a place of compassion. Compassion expands our heart and brings us closer to who we are meant to be.

Acceptance leads to suffering which births compassion... interesting concept, isn't it?

So next time you hear yourself saying, "It should be this way," understand you are creating suffering for yourself. You are not accepting things as they are right now. And if you could shift your thinking just a tad off "center," you may suffer for a little, but in the end you would find peace and compassion.

Be Selfish

If our purpose as spiritual beings living a human experience is to serve, what do you think stops us? Besides the illusion that we don't have the time, money, or resources to help others, what else do you think keeps us from living our spiritual purpose of serving others?

Getting caught up in petty human issues is one thing that keeps you from helping others. How can you possibly make a difference with devastating oil spills, horrific tsunami aftermath, starving children, and AIDS when you can't get past the argument you had with your boss today?

Struggling with your less than perfect self can keep you from helping others. How can you possibly help others when you're so messed up? "Oh my, I just have so many issues, I couldn't possibly offer up anything to anyone else right now. I mean, what do I have to offer? Really? And honestly, don't they already know all this stuff? What can I share that other people don't already know?"

Guess what? They don't know it all, and yes, you have a ton to offer the world, and the best part is that you CAN share even if you are "messed up." Personal growth is a lifelong journey. If you wait until you have it all figured out, you'll be dead.

The concept goes something like this: We are all living and playing our roles in this game of life. We are meant to learn, to struggle, to rejoice, to suffer, to love, and to get up and do it all over again every single day. Why? Because that is the human experience.

But we are more our Self if we take time to rejuvenate and fill up our Self that gets run over by the ego each day. A little "mommy-time" is what I call it, but you can call it whatever you want.

So be selfish and take some time to SEE your ego creating issues that you don't need to deal with. Take some time to STOP your ego from taking over and let your Self run the show.

RECOGNIZE the urge to live happily and follow it. NOTICE your Self— that bright inner version of You— and rejuvenate it. Heal old wounds, cry about old hurts, rest when you need to; do whatever it takes to fill up your tank so you can get out there and heal the world with your gifts.

All of us have gifts to give… let go of your fear and allow them to shine! The world needs you NOW!

Rearview Mirror

I once heard a saying that you can't move forward in your life until you stop looking in the rearview mirror. I thought it was interesting to really think about this metaphorically… of course!

You need your rearview mirror to drive right, to know and understand what's going on behind you. But it doesn't drive you. It is just the background that

you glance into every now and again to see what's there. It doesn't even impact your decisions really; it's just there for information. Do you agree?

You also need your side view mirrors to notice what's happening around you, to be aware of any obstacles that may keep you from turning or merging safely. But that's about all they do—just help with guidance, right?

So it would be appropriate then to say that driving a car is like driving your life. You need your past and your present to shape your future. You need the perspective of that rearview mirror to truly understand where you are going. And those visions in your side view mirrors… they are the beauty of your present; they are the gifts that show up in the people, circumstances, and environments that are keeping you on course right now.

Feel free, look into the rearview mirror every now and again. Take a look at your past. Try not to judge it though. You can't do anything about it… it's gone. But you need it to understand who you are and who you are becoming. Bless it… every single speed bump, turn, dead end, and winding road… it's all on your journey of life. You can be thankful for every bit of it because it has brought you to where you are right now. Which by the way is Divinely perfect!

Purification

For those of you who have not yet studied the Yoga Sutras, purification is a word you see often throughout the text. The sanskrit term is Saucha, meaning purity of mind, body, and spirit.

I could go deeply into this topic and talk about everything that creates impurities within your spiritual being. You could analyze how many impure thoughts run through your mind each day. Or how your environment really has an effect on your purity, no matter how hard you try to remain clean and clear. Or how what you put in your mouth, what you read, and what you watch on television affects you on a cellular and spiritual level… but I won't.

Not here anyway. No, this topic is a little more lighthearted. I am reminded now of a passage in the Yoga Sutras:

> *Accepting pain as help for purification, study of spiritual books, and surrender to the Supreme Being constitute yoga in practice.* – II-1

The passage talks about accepting all pain that comes to you, even though the nature of the mind is to run after pleasure. When you are offered opportunities to experience pain and suffering, you are meant to embrace those experiences because you know that they have a purifying effect on the body, mind, and the spirit and on the other side lies clarity and knowing.

Anyone who has experienced loss, disappointment, or grief gets this, right? On the other side is contentment; peace with what is. And if you are awake enough, you will say later, "Wow, I needed that pain to get to where I am now." Then you can bless that experience and move on.

So then why, while I am in Camel pose, with my heart wide open and my throat vibrating with energy, did I come out of the pose ready to burst out laughing? I seriously had to lie there as still as possible and force myself to stop laughing out loud! I was chuckling so hard that the instructor coughed a little and then moved us into the pose again! And I laughed again!

That pose used to make me cry like a baby. Hard sobs used to come from my gut which made me very hesitant to perform Camel pose when I knew it was coming up. So why the laughter?

Because laughter can be a form of purification too. We don't always have to experience pain and suffering to "come out on the other side." Pain and suffering is unavoidable I agree. However, laughter is sometimes the best medicine. And purifying laughter is not to be confused with a fake laugh designed to make people think you are "fine" with everything. I'm talking real laughter that you feel in your heart.

Laughter cleanses the heart by eradicating blockages that keep it from experiencing true love, compassion, joy, and bliss. Your heart doesn't always have to break in order to be broken open. A good laugh can do the same thing.

You may have to cry a few times before you get to the laughter but I promise, it's there!

Ignorance is Bliss

How many times have you said, "Ignorance is bliss"? Is it really? I'm not sure I believe that anymore. Now let me ask you, how many times have you said, "Boy I wish I knew then what I know now?"

Don't you think those two statements contradict each other? Yes, they do. We don't want to know, but later wish we did. Sounds silly, right? That's part of being human I suppose!

I have heard living life ignorantly is sort of like being one of those balls in a pinball machine. Just letting the pressure of life PUSH us into the "game" of life and then bouncing around, aimlessly, trying not to fall into the trap of oblivion that ends our game.

And then, we get another chance! Because NOW we know how to tilt our body just so to avoid that one hurdle, only to miss the one that came out from nowhere and dropped us back into oblivion.

The thing about pinball is we get, if I remember correctly, three chances. In life we get many more. In fact, we keep getting chances until we finally get it right! And by getting it right I mean we feel, think, and act in a way that is in alignment with our soul—blissful, if you will!

So ask yourself if you really want to live in ignorance. I'm not saying you have to know it all in order to navigate through life. But wouldn't it be nice to say, "I am open to the lessons I am to learn every day so that I may live from a place that is more in alignment with my soul"?

Ignorance is bliss says, "I don't want to know about it… I don't want to deal with it… I don't want to grow."

Believe me, life gives us the lessons we are meant to learn every moment. There is really no room for ignorance, to be honest. Educate yourself just

enough on the topics that are right for your heart and your life will continue to hand you bliss!

Connection

I struggled this week with what to write about… can you believe it? And then I thought, as I drifted off to sleep, just last night, "Of course… this is so important to me! Why haven't I written about it before?"

Connection… with your family, friends, children, others, your work, your environment, the earth, your soul. Connection is so important to us all even if we don't admit it. We may think that we could care less about if we are connected or not, but that's a lie we tell ourselves when we have sunken into isolation.

Examples: You tell yourself that you are right so you don't have to say you are sorry and connect with someone else. You go to work half-heartedly, just to "get through the day." You wish for something different in your life: a different home, car or neighborhood, instead of connecting and loving the movie YOU created for yourself. You think that your choice of not recycling, composting, or making earth-friendly choices isn't going to make a difference anyway, so why do it? And you occupy yourself so much that you don't make time to connect with your own spirit… ever. You just keep going along your human experience until you feel like you are all alone.

Connection is at the root of your soul. It's why you are here. Everyone yearns for connection at their deepest level. No one wants to live in isolation…no one. The only reason we deprive ourselves of connection with others is out of fear of getting hurt or fear of losing ourselves. Think about it. When you are most upset with a family member, a partner, or another person, what's at the root? Connection. They don't understand you, there isn't enough time, they aren't listening, you can't express yourself properly… it's almost AL-WAYS about connecting.

We all want to connect, but our ego has built this shield to protect our soul from connection. It's the way the ego survives. So in times of perceived danger, we shut down. We adamantly proclaim that we are right, we push emotional relationships away with a wave of our hand, we proclaim we don't need anymore friends, we walk around with our head down, we don't smile at strangers!

And with the way technology continues to grow, I don't see it getting any better unless we make an effort. And I mean it. I walked off a plane awhile back and every single person in the lobby was staring down at their phones and texting away. Just the other night, at my attempt to work myself back into the single life, I went to a local bar with friends. Almost every person at the bar was texting … stay home for Pete's sake and text! I laughed out loud. Seriously? What is so damn important? Do you REALLY have to be doing something every single second? Maybe if we looked up every now and again, we may notice someone who needs help, or the beauty of a couple in love, or we may—gulp— be silent with our thoughts. Ooh… that's scary!

We are going to be a society of heartless, hunched-over people with respiratory issues, heart issues, and arthritis in our necks and our fingers if we aren't careful.

LOOK UP, people! LOOK AROUND YOU! Acknowledge the people around you. LOVE the life you live, live the life you LOVE. Take five minutes to breathe and then walk into work with a new perspective. Turn the phone off, for heaven's sake. Say you are sorry. LOOK at your child when they are talking to you! NONE of this other stuff is going to matter when you get older. It's not. In fact, this may be all you get, so connect NOW.

It's all so easy, isn't it? Connection is imperative to our soul. Don't let the ego and technology stop this flow. It's what the world is about. We are one, we want to connect, we want to acknowledge and KNOW that we are all a part of each other and this earth. This is a big one, I know. But it's very important for the survival of our species… connection. I don't care how you do it today, just do it.

Issues in Your Tissues

People venture into a yoga class mainly for the physical aspects of the practice. They complain about tight hips and hamstrings, lower back pain, sciatic pain, and too much stress. This is why most people attend a yoga class. And I love it! Because yoga is like a tricky little trap. It reels you in with a promise of reduced stress and anxiety, increased strength and flexibility, and a calmer disposition. Who wouldn't want that, especially now when life moves so fast!

What most beginners don't understand is what is going on beneath the surface in an asana class. Honestly, I am a little reluctant to let this secret out for fear of YOU not coming to class, but here goes.

When you move your body in a yoga class, what is actually happening is movement of the issues in your tissues. What does that mean? Physically, it means that when you hold a posture for more than 60 seconds, and then you go deeper into that posture, combined with slow rhythmic breathing, you actually access the areas of the body below the muscle, below the bone, into the fascia, and even into the subtle, energy body.

Whoa… what does that mean? Sounds invasive, right?

This phenomenon is why sometimes you cry or laugh in a posture. Because you have gotten so deep into the body that you have accessed buried information. So let's say you are in a deep, deep Humble Warrior. And you are literally starting to cramp a little. The question is, are you really cramping or is your mind telling you, "Come out of this posture now. You may lose it in a second."

Yogis talk about their "edge" in a posture. This is what your "edge" can look like.

It's not necessarily painful, but it is uncomfortable. And usually it's the same "uncomfortable-ness" you feel all the time, in the same poses, and in the

same area of the body. It's blocked energy that has been there for a long, long time.

Now, I don't want to discount physical injuries or the fact that you may be tight in certain areas BECAUSE of your lifestyle of sitting. However, I also can't ignore the fact that most people live a fast-paced life; one that requires us to be on the go all the time. Not only that but every one of us buries or holds onto pain.

From childhood and way into the present moment, we hold onto pain. Depending upon what it is: fear, guilt, shame, grief, lies, illusion or attachment, we ALL harbor these emotions in our body. And they LIVE in our tissues.

So I ask you this one question. How can you TRULY be living a life you love when you are holding onto this old stuff? Can you REALLY be living your most authentic, purposeful life when you are holding onto this crud; or is your life a façade? Something to think about: what is real and what is an illusion of happiness. And how can you get to the REAL stuff?

Only one answer, three words:... breathe... move... awaken. That's it. And if you are scared, come another day. But just a forewarning: Once you DO come to class and you get that taste of cells and energy moving, AND you can all of a sudden touch your toes, you will want to come back over and over again. It will become who you are.

Moving Past the Edge

In class I talk a lot about moving past your "edge" in a pose. You know that spot... when you feel your leg starting to cramp, your arms getting as heavy as bricks, that same kink in your lower back start to ache. It's that moment when you say, "I gotta get out of this pose now!" and then immediately, you do. You pull out of the pose and find a more comfortable variation.

Now, let me preface this by saying that I have always shared the physical practice of yoga from a place of compassion, options, and modifications to fit every body. However, I have also, over the last few years, experienced the real power of yoga. And while I still believe that yoga is for "every body", and that you can make a pose "fit your body," I also believe that each of us comes to our mat to move beyond our comfort level—and we can.

So starting with the physical practice (which it ALWAYS does...), what happens when you stay in one variation of the pose? You become stagnant, that's what happens. You don't get stronger, leaner or more open; you stay right where you are. In fact, you may even purposefully hold yourself back from moving forward or challenging yourself (if you even come to class at all).

The monkey mind says things like, "Oh, here it comes, that pain in my neck always starts right here. I better just hold back so it doesn't hurt again," or "Maybe next week I'll try to bring my forehead to my knee," or "I just KNOW I'm not strong enough to try Bakasana (Crow Pose); I'll just sit and watch everyone else." And even more interesting, "Man I'm thirsty. I'm going to stop (which happens at the same time/pose/variation every single class) and take a drink of water."

This is what the ego does; it keeps you in the familiar. Why? Because it's a safer choice—it preserves your current reality.

The mind is programed to STOP, LAY OFF, or AVOID when discomfort sets in. But the truth is discomfort (not to be confused with searing, hot pain) is good! It's a signal from the body it's time to move past what you have been holding onto for days/weeks/months/ years. And when you are talking about your yoga asana practice, it shows up as discomfort in a muscle or joint or fear of going upside down, for example. You continue to baby it, hold onto it, feed it with sympathy, and use it as an excuse not to move forward.

What would it be like if you moved past that discomfort? What would happen if you pushed yourself just a bit past your edge in a pose? What are you afraid of? Falling on your face? Hurting yourself? Growth? A higher set of expectations?

But what would it feel like to get past that edge with breath? With focus and intention? Do you know? Have you tried it? I can tell you... IT'S INCREDIBLE and VERY liberating and empowering. To go upside down for the first time brings you back to childlike bliss.

So now, as always, take this experience off your mat. Where are you holding back in your life? Why are you not teetering on the edge at least once a year? Scary thought, yes? Are you complacent in your day-to-day choices? Are you living a life that is less than what you could be living because it's safe? Because it's familiar?

Because the fear of loneliness, isolation, poverty, and finding nothing that compares to the life you are already living takes over anytime you think you could be, do, or contribute more? Because the people who are in your life right now represent stability, security, and a clear path? Because the pattern of resisting something new is easier than going for it full-throttle?

Stretch your mind. We are One. You will never be lonely, you will never be isolated, you will never be poor. The edge may be scary to peer over some days… it may seem like a long way down. But think of it as growth and opportunity instead, incorporate this new belief into a daily mantra for yourself.

"Bring on the wonder… bring on the bliss… let me stretch my mind beyond what I think possible. Let my "reality" shift to something I cannot even imagine for myself. Allow me the faith and openness I need to fully stretch my mind so my heart can open."

Whoa… try that one on for size. What do YOU come up with?

Surrender

Every time I teach a class, I summon an intention to lead with. I don't search for it, I don't try to think of something, I just let inspiration come to me and usually it does. But when I went to class this one particular morning, I went blank! I kept thinking, How am I going to lead class? I have no intention today!

And then as I sat there, with everyone in Child's Pose, the word surrender came up. And as I looked out at the fall weather, the trees waving in the wind, their leaves falling off aimlessly, it totally came to me.

What does surrender really mean? Does it mean that we give up? That we say, "Whatever will be, will be?" or "I guess I will never… do that pose, get that job, live my life the way I want, be happy…" whatever your end of the sentence may be.

Well sort of, but not really.

Does it mean that we completely let go of all attachment to everything we know just so life can happen to us?

Well, kind of, but not really.

I noticed the fall trees on this particular day and realized that they offer the perfect example of surrender. They have been here, potentially for lifetimes. They are completely rooted into the Earth; grounded into their space, in their Being, and they understand their ability to contribute to this world. They know their place and their role and they play it very well.

When fall comes and their leaves begin to turn colors, they begin to transform and take on an entirely different look. They transform. And the funny thing is they don't ever resist this natural cycle of fall and the seasons changing. You know what I mean? They don't fight the laws of nature by not allowing their leaves to fall. They don't cling to their leaves hoping that if they stay the same then everything will be all right. They don't fight this natural transformation… this is what happens. Not only do they surrender, but they look so beautiful letting go. They represent surrender with grace.

They are confident in the ebb and flow of life. They know that they will lose their leaves; they will become bare and have to rely on their inner resources to stay warm during the colder months. They prepare for this transformation gracefully through the fall months and stand tall during winter.

And when spring comes, they bloom so beautifully. In fact, most times they come out on the other side more radiant than the prior year. They do this with faith and confidence that this is the way that it is… and it can't possibly be any other way.

Nature happens… it's law. If we could learn to surrender to our own life's impermanence, knowing beyond all knowing that this "fall" will bring more beauty and radiance on the other side, we would be just like the trees.

Let go, surrender, and let nature take its course with your life. Be firm in your ground, but open to the beauty within. It is always more gorgeous in the spring, but you have to go through fall and winter to get there.

Conscious Choices

How many decisions do you make in one day? The answer is simple: you make decisions every moment of every day… most likely thousands of times a day. Now, those decisions can range from simple things like what to eat, what to wear, and which way to turn. They can also be complex; for example, how to react in any given situation, how to answer an inquisitive child, or how to better your life. No matter how simple or complex the choice, every decision directs your life. And you can direct your life consciously or unconsciously. Your thoughts create your day, your week, your year, and eventually your life.

On average, how present do you think you are when you make those decisions? On average, would you say that all of your decisions are made from a place of grace and thoughtfulness? How about half of them? A quarter?

Try only about ten percent of them.

How's that for a big fat gulp? You make more unconscious decisions… actually, let me rephrase that. Your ego makes more decisions about your life than your Self does. It's no wonder how on some days you may look at your life and say, "How in the world did I get here?"

The reality is that you make many unconscious decisions all day, every day that lead you down a path that isn't really authentic.

Thoughts become things... every single time... so how can you make your thoughts more powerful and consciously directed? You find space for grace... space between thought and reaction.

Grace happens in those moments when you consciously choose how to think, how to react, what to eat, and what to DO in your life that is exactly in alignment with your soul. How will you know you made space for grace? Time will move slowly, you will hear yourself breathing.

I'm telling you, it's ALL YOGA! It's ALL BREATH! When you don't use breath and yoga, you walk around asleep like the majority of society, making decisions that are NOT in alignment with who you are. Most people are just "getting by," just "surviving," just wondering: "When is my life going to change?" The question they don't ask is "What is necessary for this change?"

More space for grace is necessary! Space where you breathe and connect to that Universal Oneness. Space where you are making decisions from a conscious, loving place, and ONLY concerned with the well-being of your Self.

GASP... isn't that selfish? No, it's really not. Because if you believe that we are all One and you act in a way that is concerned with the well-being of your Self, you are ultimately concerned with the well-being of the whole.

You don't need to change the world; stop trying to change the world. Just make conscious choices for your Self (with a capital S by the way) and you will witness exponential changes and shifts for yourself and the world you are currently watching.

Connecting to the Earth

This past week, I was fortunate enough to head to the beach for three days and write. It's funny because I could easily write at home, in my slippers and pajamas by the fire, but that picture doesn't work given the fact that I have two kids, an abundant life, and other "real life" responsibilities that take precedence over connecting with my inner voice.

It just doesn't work that way right now.

So I take matters into my own hands, because I know the importance of completing this book. Not so much for all of you, but for myself, really. And I go to the beach. This is where I connect.

And I know this because when I get to the beach, the heavens open up, the waves crash, the weather turns from gray skies to blue and everything, I mean EVERYTHING is Divinely guided.

I have always been connected to the ocean. There is just something about it that really pulls at my soul. I am not sure if it is the waves and the mystery with how they move. Maybe it's the sound they make when they crash along the shore. Or maybe it's just the fact that they consistently flow, never stopping, without anyone telling them what to do or how to do it. They just keep flowing.

Whatever it is, it's bigger than me and incomprehensible. It's a miracle, really. Add in windswept trees, eroding cliffs, seagulls chilling, whales moving south, and people watching this movie in awe, and I've got one amazing place to hear my heart.

So what I thought of while I was at the beach is this: Know where you connect to your soul. It may not be in your home, amidst "real life." You connect there, but you are also swept away with "real life." Where do you connect to your heart?

I know it's somewhere in nature, because at your soul level you know that you are just like nature. You are ever-changing, you are a miracle, you enjoy flowing along with what will be, and you know, at your deepest level of knowing that in nature, you see you Self. Nature is Divinely guided and doesn't need a map to tell it where to go and neither do you.

Find your space in nature, wherever it may be, and get there… as often as you can. Recharge, plug in, and fill up. It's so amazingly worth it.

In the Dark

Have you ever hit a point in your life where everything seems like it's totally out of control? When every aspect of your life is upside down, sideways, backward, and very unfamiliar?

I equate it to when the lights go out unexpectedly. You know what that's like, right? That feeling you get the second it gets pitch black and you can't see a thing? Your stomach drops and your heart beats faster. You look around, knowing that you can't see anything, but you look around anyway expecting to see something! Then you try to remember where you put the flashlight, if it has batteries in it, where the candles are, if you have a lighter, and then you think, when are the lights going to come back on?

I know it can be challenging to appreciate any benefit to walking around in the dark, bumping into things. In the dark, it's hard to see where you are going, whether or not you are alone, and what your next step should be. It may even be impossible to imagine how darkness, loss of control, and confusion can be helpful. Maybe you have always been afraid of the dark. But why are you afraid? Because you can't see anything, there is a huge unknown, and you have no control.

Being in the dark is similar to the feeling you experience when you lose your job; your relationship begins to unravel; your house loses its value; your bank account is lower than it's ever been; your business begins failing; you are forced to file bankruptcy; you fall out of love; a family member's health begins declining; your health starts to decline; your truth and everything you have known up until now has changed and everything you believed is in question. You are in the dark and confused about what is real and what is illusion.

The lights of your life are out, nothing makes sense, you've got to change it and gain control... NOW!

Sound familiar?

The truth is that during times of darkness and uncertainty, everything becomes crystal clear. How can that be? Because all along you thought you had control: control of your "destiny" and that illusion of control has been your mantra your entire life. When the lights go out, that illusion is ripped out from underneath you.

Control is an illusion. You don't have control of anything... except of course your perception. When you change your perception, you can open the door for spiritual growth and awakening. As long as you are here on Earth, you are GOING to have to face times of uncertainty and darkness. How are you going to handle it? Are you going to be afraid or are you going to embrace it?

We rely so much on our eyes to understand, but they really create an optical illusion of what is going on in our life. Our sight is based on perceptions, experiences, and judgments. Our eyes, or the perceptions of our ego, create detours and obstacles that keep us from living our higher purpose. Our ego is afraid of the dark... it needs the light and judgment in order to know where to go.

In contrast, the soul feels and our truth is only defined from within our heart. The soul actually needs darkness in order to move toward its higher purpose. The soul, our heart, loves the dark... in fact it navigates better in the darkness.

How about you redefine darkness to mean awe-inspiring and awakening? What if you walked through the darkness and it brought you to the light? What if the unknown was more beautiful and peaceful than you could

imagine? What if there was no resistance in the unknown? What if the unknown was everything you had imagined for yourself and more blissful than you ever thought possible?

This space is necessary for growth, for personal evolution. We need this space in order to hear our heart. We need this space to remember to have faith in the things we cannot see. So embrace the darkness. When life starts to hand you times of uncertainty... stop... breathe... close your eyes and really take it all in. It's your soul, begging to be heard. Listen and begin navigating the path of your life from your soul. Go into the darkness... it always leads to the light.

Three Answers

Isn't it funny how when you are searching for an answer to something, it comes to you so unbelievably fast? It just takes one authentic plea for clarity, reasoning, or understanding, and boom, the Universe provides it, lickety-split!

We all do it; we all ask for something on a daily basis. We all "pray" in some way, shape, or form. You make plans, trying to control the outcome so it fits nicely into your life. You are certain that you know what's best. You assume that you are in the driver's seat of your life and boy, when it doesn't go your way, you fight it.

You resist it, you blame, you get angry and you push against the Universe with a vengeance. You wonder why? You search for another way... you continue to try things to make it work out your way. You are living from a place of fear when you do this. You are afraid of what you can't see. You are so scared that if things don't work out exactly how YOU planned, that life will fall apart.

But I'm telling you that's not how it is. In fact, it's just the opposite. Continue to make your plans… go for it! But remember this when life throws you a curveball: the Universe only has three answers to your prayers:

> Yes.

> Not now.

> I have something better in mind.

The answer is never no… never.

Do you believe that? If you don't… if you feel burdened by life and the cards it hands you, open your heart. I swear to you, the Universe is trying to get in, but for some reason you are choosing not to open up. Your mind is filled with ideas that you have to "figure it all out" and you "need" to get it all together and your efforts will equal perfection in the Universe.

That's crazy! You don't own that much responsibility and power! Nor do you want it!

Just try this: breathe in as deep as you can and then when you exhale, have your body go limp. Feel as if every muscle, ligament, joint, tendon, and bone is dropping to the floor. Imagine all the resistance and tension in your body melting. Now equate that to your thoughts. Let your "ideas" about what should be happening in your life right now go. Open up to the possibility that for some reason, you are supposed to experiencing whatever it is and that it's about to break you open to a new dimension of who you are and how you view the life you are living.

Ah… now, isn't that much nicer?

How Will You Show Up?

Do you hear yourself talk each day? What do you say? Can you witness your body language when communicating with others? Do you stop and breathe between every thought and reaction? Do you honestly observe every thought that runs through your mind each day? Can you name the emotion(s) that run through your mind when you think a thought or speak a word?

For most of us, the answer to every single one of those questions is "no." You may have this type of "awakening" once during the day, maybe a few times if you're intentional about it. But most of us aren't conscious enough in our daily activities to really observe our Self in action. We just move throughout our day in a semi-robotic state.

With approximately 70,000 thoughts in our head and more information at our fingertips in a day than people only 100 years ago had in their lifetime, we almost have to fall "asleep" for a little while so we can survive!

But what would the world look like if you DID hear yourself talk each day? What if you could take a breath every single time before you spoke? What would you think if you saw your body language when relating to others? Visualize a camera following you around all day long. How would that tape look when you were reviewing it later? After getting over the awkwardness of it all, are there some edits, deletes, and retakes you may hope for?

We all would.

What if I told you that all you needed to do, in order to begin this "witnessing" process, was to take a yoga class? Would you try it? Stepping on your yoga mat is the perfect place to evaluate how you show up in the world on any given day. It's not that you are judging yourself, per se; however, if you really want to observe how you navigate in this world, get on a yoga mat.

Notice where you place your mat in the room. And then, when you go back to class for more, do you go right to that same spot? Or do you choose a different one? What do you bring into class with you? Your water? Your watch? A towel? Your phone? How many "necessities" do you really need?

Then notice, are you breathing? How are you breathing? Full or shallow? How often do you think of something else besides your breath? Or how your body feels in any given pose? How often do you run through your task list or your grocery list?

Here comes the fun stuff: Do you compare yourself to others? Are you watching everyone else? What thoughts run through your mind then? How about when you approach a pose that is challenging for you? What do you do? Stop? Reach for your water? Force yourself into it? What do you do?

How about when the instructor says, "Find stillness in Mountain Pose." Do you fidget? And the ever elusive Savasana (Corpse Pose) at the end of class. Ah… this is where it all happens. How do you show up in Corpse Pose? Do you scratch your nose, wiggle your toes, move around? Does your mind wander? Do you count the minutes in your mind, waiting for the instructor to give you permission to get up?

These are all just ideas for you to play with. And honestly, they are all things I used to do when I first stepped onto my mat many years ago. So don't judge yourself or shy away from yoga. Just try it and see. See how you show up and then when you go out into the world you will have a different perspective on how you navigate your life.

You may even shift your course a little with this awakening! You may actually be able to breathe, stop fidgeting, and show up exactly as your soul intends!

Dedication vs. Obsession

During Eagle Pose in class one day, the instructor was addressing the new people and she said, "We have some very dedicated practitioners here in the front row. They are great examples of what the pose can look like." When she said that, I almost burst out laughing. Not because of what she said, but how my mind interpreted it. I had been staring at myself so intently in the mirror, not from an ego standpoint, but from a survival standpoint, and my mind fixated on her statement.

Was it dedication that brought me to class at 6 a.m. three days a week or was it obsessiveness?

I mean, really, how do you distinguish between an obsessive behavior and a dedicated practice? A few ideas came to me throughout the rest of my practice that morning so I thought I would share.

In my opinion, when you are obsessed with something— an exercise routine, your yoga practice, a clean house, the way people perceive you, or the way you think things should be—you are focused on the outcome. You are expecting a certain outcome from your behavior. You exercise with the intent on losing a certain amount of inches around your waist. You go to yoga for a more flexible body or a calmer mind. You clean the house because someone important is coming to visit and you want the house to look just right. You speak in a way that you hope will bring about acceptance from others. You are focused on the outcome... not the act itself... the outcome.

And most of the time, obsessing with an outcome brings about less than desirable results... disappointment, anger, resentment. You keep doing what you are doing expecting a certain outcome which we have all experienced at some point, right?

But just for fun, let's say your obsessiveness "pays off." Let's say that you lose those inches, you gain flexibility, you find inner peace, your mother-in-law thinks your house looks great, and people invite you to lots of parties. Then what? What's wrong with obsessiveness then?

Because the euphoria you feel is short-lived. It's an immediate ego-boosting rush that fulfills a moment in time. It's a disillusioned perception that the ego needs to continue to survive. Acceptance, approval, recognition… all those things are ego-driven so the ego obsesses toward an outcome.

Dedication, on the other hand, is when you act in a way that serves your soul. Taking the same examples from above, you exercise because you feel good in that moment. You go to yoga because you experience the connection between your mind, body, and soul even for a fleeting moment. You clean your house because you love how you feel without so much clutter. And you speak in a way that resonates with your truth regardless of what other people think.

You are dedicated to your soul's evolution beyond the ego. You are dedicated to the feeling behind a moment during your actions. You are dedicated to understanding the power of your actions without attachment to the outcome. You are not concerned with an outcome because you understand that all you have is this moment.

I am happy to conclude that dedication is what brings me to yoga every day. It's those little moments when I break through a physical limitation or mental block that keep me free from obsessing.

Affirmations & Postures

Have faith to stretch your mind so your heart can open.

Living your bliss is what we are meant to be, do, and feel. And gratitude is the powerhouse that gives you the inspiration to get there.

Nature is Divinely guided. It doesn't need a map to tell it what to do; neither do you.

Find your space in nature and get there as often as you can. Recharge, plug in and fill up.

Stay true to that which you believe and your life will unfold as it should. Listen to your heart and it will always speak your truth.

I choose love. I choose cooperation. I choose Oneness.

Laughter cleanses the heart by eradicating blockages that keep it from experiencing true love, compassion, joy, and bliss. Your heart doesn't always have to break in order to be broken open. A good laugh can do the same thing.

Anahata

Bow

Camel

Cobra

Cowface

Dancers

Reverse Warrior

Fish

Chapter 5
On Lies versus Truth
Throat Chakra: Vishuddha

Graceful Intentions

I have always thought of life as a smorgasbord. Not only that, but I also still believe that when you desire something, you simply shuffle your energy toward it and it becomes your reality.

I still believe those things; however, I have softened a little... but only a little.

So for the sake of collective understanding here, can you agree that we are all energy? And can you further agree that we all create our own reality? And can you also agree that we can change our perception and our life as we see it right now with just our thoughts?

Assuming all this is correct, then it would seem simple enough to just manifest, right? Manifest that loving relationship, the perfect job, fulfilling life, and financial abundance, right?

I could go in so many directions with this one, but I will keep it super simple and try not to run off on a tangent.

When you state an intention about what you desire, the most important thing is clarity. And honestly, it is just as important to find the proper balance of attention on that which you wish to manifest. This is where I want to focus with this Om: on the proper balance of attention in the process of manifestation... graceful intentions.

Keep in mind that when you "manifest," it isn't about reaching a "goal," per se. So drop the word "goal." Reaching for a goal means you have work to do to get to a certain point.

Instead, when you manifest, you state an intention and then you ask for guidance and protection while you go about your way to your intention. You are telling the Universe that you have a desire, but you know that you can't control everything, so please Universe, help guide you.

So... you state it, you daydream about it, you visualize it, and then you say

something like, "I am open to this as I dream it to be… or something better." You say "I am open to the gifts and challenges that will bring me to this manifestation." Remember, the gifts aren't always beautifully wrapped…but you have to be open to them all.

I call this setting Graceful Intentions. You can be a goal-setting, intentional individual, but remember that there is something bigger than all of us. Let's honor that and ask for guidance…every single day.

The Dreadlock

I have to tell this story because it's so unbelievably funny I couldn't stand it. Let me preface this by reminding you that the Universe is moving faster, resulting in instant manifestation. When we think a thought or speak a word, instantly the Universe delivers that to us. Confused? What that means is our life is instantaneously reflecting back to us what we think, feel, and do. And if you have any question or hesitation about that, breathe more during your day and witness everything coming to you exactly according to your thoughts. But be prepared…you will learn some huge lessons about who you really are during this process.

The other day I was brushing Isabella's hair (my older daughter) because she wanted pigtails. I got frustrated with her because she had these crazy knots in the lower layer of her hair. They were obviously from not brushing her hair like I had asked her to do a thousand times before. Pay attention here before you judge…

So we argued and went through this whole mother-daughter struggle about her hair. The drama that followed was smoothed over in the car ride to school. But, much to my surprise, the very next day, I was washing my hair and I felt this HUGE knot, no… DREADLOCK in the back of my own hair! NEVER have I ever had a dreadlock… EVER! But then again, I never brush my hair out properly either.

I laughed…out loud. And I realized in that instant, the Universe wanted to remind me of a few things:

- I set the example not by what I say, but by what I do.

- I am not in control of my daughter's hair; she is.

- She will learn when she has to take scissors to her hair and cut out her own knot.

- I am not perfect, so stop acting like it.

- Pick the battles that are important.

- It's beneficial to be vulnerable with your child and share where you can do better.

So…here I am again, learning from these little spirits. How blessed I am to be part of their journey and open to all that they have to teach me. Just for the record, Isabella was oddly proud when I showed her how much hair I had to cut off to get that knot out.

Forward Flexion

I have come to believe that for most people, life is a forward motion of energy. For some people, the illusion is that they can move that energy in a direction they control. Let me be more specific: Most Westerners live their lives in a constant state of flexion—or forward movement. For a second, consider the way you walk. Most likely, you walk with purpose, your head in front of your heart, almost always straining forward from your neck.

Here's another example I think everyone can relate to. Generally, think about how you strain over your computer, hunched over and closed off at the hips. Physically speaking, this simple posture of hunching over your computer

seals off the flow of energy in your hips (sacral chakra—natural flow of plea-surable energy), closes off the energy of your abdominals (solar plexus—the energy that directs your purpose), constricts the heart and lungs (heart chakra—place of love, connection, and compassion), deflates the shoulders and neck (throat chakra—your sense of creative expression)... ultimately disconnecting you from your higher power of being and aliveness, that belief in Universal guidance (third eye and crown chakra—the connection we share with all beings and all that IS).

As a human being, you ask how, why, when. You create your life based on perceptions, fears, and beliefs that come from your ego mind. You uncon-sciously close yourself off to the greater powers of being that are truly guid-ing you behind the scenes of your life.

That doesn't sound like fun if you ask me. In fact, it sounds like the total op-posite of why I chose to incarnate in this life. Does it really have to be that way? Do you really think you have to work that hard to "make life happen?" What if you allowed your heart to usher you forward instead? If you said, "I trust," or "I love," or "I believe." What then?

What would your life look like then? If you could just wake up and ask, "What is my highest good today?" or "How can I give and grow today?" or "What am I meant to experience today?" These types of questions come from the soul, from the heart—from our innermost authentic being.

Let your heart lead you today. If you have already begun your day in state of forward flexion, you can start over. Close your eyes and breathe into that spaciousness of your heart. It's infinite, it's limitless... the power of love and compassion come naturally to you. YOU block it off... YOU close it... YOU get caught up in the other "stuff." Let it go and breathe. Watch your heart usher you forward. It's an awesome rush.

Secret Thoughts

Think you can keep a secret? Maybe you can from a standpoint of not telling someone something. Sure. But what about keeping a secret about your feelings or your true desires? Can you do that? Can you think one thing, but speak or act in a completely different way?

The answer is no, you cannot.

How do I know this? Because no matter what you say, your thoughts create the movie of your life. When you think a thought, it goes out into the Universe and sends out a beacon of interest. From that beacon of interest, people and situations start magnetizing to that thought. And that thought is like a ricochet… it comes right back to you.

Now the question is, do you grab hold of those people or situations when they come back to you or do you ignore the signs? Most likely you grab hold of them… most likely unconsciously, but maybe consciously… depending upon how "awake" you are to this thought you have. Then you build upon the thought again and it gets sent out into the Universe again, only to rebound back to you AGAIN and show up as your life.

The Universe wants nothing more than for you to get exactly what you want. And it starts with your thoughts. When your thoughts don't match your speech or your actions, the Universe gets a little confused.

It sends you people and circumstances that represent both your thoughts and your actions. It can get very confusing… usually when you are harboring secret thoughts and living in a totally different light, your life becomes chaotic and overwhelming.

This doesn't mean you are a hypocrite, a liar, a fraud, or a fake. It means your physical body hasn't caught up with your soul yet… that's all. It means that your ego is still driving, but NOW the soul is tired of being in the backseat. Your soul begins speaking up in a whisper.

So my suggestion is… explore your secret thoughts in depth. Share them with one or two people you feel close to. Say them out loud so you can hear yourself say them! See how that feels. Then you have to decide… are your secret thoughts real or are they based in the ego or the soul? Only you can feel that one truth… and stay out of the mind on this one. Use the heart instead.

Creative Expression

How do you creatively express yourself? Do you have a passion for creating anything at all? When was the last time you created something that was uniquely YOU? In high school? Grade school? Kindergarten? Do you KNOW what makes your heart sing in divine creation?

Everyone has a natural-born talent or divine creative expression… even YOU! There is something that you LOVE doing, creating, or being. If you don't know what it is, it's most likely buried underneath responsibility, obligations, outside perceptions, judgments, or fear.

So let me ask you again… how do YOU creatively express yourself? How do you use that creative side of your brain and offer your gifts and talents to the world? Do you know what you are good at? Do you know what you love to do?

No?

Then stop. Close your eyes and visualize yourself with no responsibilities. That's right… knock them all out. Be free from all of them if only for just a minute or two or three. What would you do with your time if you could do anything you wanted to do? How would you express yourself from a soul level of being?

Do you like to paint? Draw? Write? Dance? Cook? Plan? Play? Sing? Organize? Connect? Speak? Act? Inspire? What IS the word that best describes you? The ideas are limitless! Everyone has a word that best describes who they are and what they love. Can you see yourself acting out that word?

We all have responsibilities and obligations. Almost everyone I know is afraid of failing and nervous about what other people might think if they follow their "big idea" or their lifelong dream. But what COULD your life look like if you followed that creative expression? WHAT IF it started as a hobby and all of sudden it was supporting you? And all of a sudden you were doing what you loved every single day?

Whoosh… that's how it works!

Squished

Feeling squished lately? Like you are being shoved or squeezed into a space where sooner or later you are going to have to burst out and say, "OK AL-READY! WHAT DO YOU WANT ME TO DO?"

Two things here… if you are feeling that way, it's because the Universe is provoking you to move forward with your life purpose. And if you are feeling squished, it's because you are not living your life purpose. Not only that, but what you are surrounding yourself with right now has nothing to do with your life purpose.

"It's time to show up" is what the Universe is telling you. You're there spiritually and maybe emotionally, but not so much physically.

This squished feeling may manifest as tight muscles, aching neck, shoulders, chest, or turbulent stomach. Sound familiar?

The other part to this squished feeling is surrendering to the fact that maybe you don't KNOW what your life purpose is. Ask yourself… do you know what it is? Don't be shy. Say, "No, I have no idea what my purpose is!"

Does it sound like this? "My life purpose is to support my family!" NOT!

"My life purpose is to make enough money to save for retirement!" NOT!

"My life purpose is to find a relationship that completes me!" NOT!

None of these statements are life purposes! Not one! So if this is where your thinking goes when someone asks you what your life purpose is, it's time to change it.

Stop the squished feeling and instead feel EXPANSION into IDEAS that promote INFINITE POSSIBILITIES.

You are feeling squished because YOU put yourself into a box. Get out of the box and start living already!

Keeping It Together

Do you hold your feelings in for the sake of keeping the peace? Do you think it's easier to put on a happy face just so others around you can think that everything is all right? When people ask you how you are, do you say, "GREAT!" when you really want to say, "I'm falling apart and I wish someone would catch me already!"

Why do you do this to yourself? Keeping it together can only go so far before the reality of your true feelings begins manifesting as pain, illness, and overall frustration. Exactly whose peace are you keeping it together for anyway? Not your own. What you are doing by holding things in is actually creating your own little hell on earth.

Not only that, but those individuals around you are pulled into your façade and aren't offered the opportunity of knowing the true YOU.

I admit, there are appropriate times to hold off from expressing anger, frustration, grief, disappointment, and anguish, especially if you are going through a life-changing shift.

But usually during those times, you are offered a pause... a moment to experience the feeling, and either choose to follow it until it's expelled completely from the body, or hold it in until it comes out as something entirely different.

Allow your feelings to flow through you so you can move that energy out. When you hold onto it, the feeling (the energy) manifests itself into negativity and it usually projects itself to others as resentment, guilt, or aggression. And how does that help the evolution of your soul?

You don't need to keep it together for anyone. Just be YOU... and you can't possibly be together all the time... can you?

Your Stories

I love this OM already and I haven't even written it yet! I am already smiling because understanding your stories is the number one way to break free from them. And believe me, you WANT to break free from them.

Let me preface this by saying that the best author I know who can free you from your stories is Byron Katie. If you read this Om and it resonates with you and you want to know more, you MUST go to her website, get her book, and do her "work." She is amazing and so is this knowledge.

Visualize this: Your stories are huge textbooks you carry around with you. Usually a single book starts off under your arm. Then the homework involved gets heavy, so you get a shoulder bag for all your stories. But eventually you start walking a little crooked and have to see a chiropractor. She recommends a backpack for all your stories. At least you will feel in alignment then. So you get a backpack to put all your stories in and eventually you are slumping over your heart and respiratory systems so much that you have to see a specialist. Now you are having trouble breathing and your heart begins to beat irregularly. This can't be good.

Now what? You HAVE to carry those stories around with you! They protect you. They sustain you! What are you going to do?

The ONLY thing you CAN do is drop the stories one by one.

You know the ones I am talking about: "My mom wasn't there for me. My dad left when I was little. My mom did everything for me... I never had to take responsibility. My dad was an alcoholic. I was raped. I was bullied. I was made fun of in school. I was molested. I never had a healthy sexual relationship. My coach told me I wasn't good enough for the A-team. My art teacher said I couldn't make money with my art. I never won a trophy playing the piano. I didn't get enough love from my parents. I was neglected. I had an abortion when I was young and never told anyone. I was fat. I was anorexic. I smoked pot. I did drugs. I cheated through high school."

STOP with the stories already! ACK! Aren't you tired of them? They're heavy, and they don't matter! They are weighing you down! They create density in your aura and keep you from being who you are meant to be! They do nothing for you except keep you rooted in the past.

Some of you aren't even aware of the stories that you are carrying around. They show up as a general unhappiness. Maybe you are going to counseling to "figure them out." Maybe you are beginning to understand where you came from. I applaud you for beginning the internal dig. But while you dig, please keep in mind that they are stories, nothing more.

They are stories based on your LIMITED PERCEPTIONS from way back when. You made judgments about your self-worth and your capabilities based on these situations. You had limited knowledge and experience about the world around you and how you fit in, so take your perceptions with a grain of salt.

You don't have to EVER understand why your mom wasn't there, your dad drank, your coach was insensitive, or you felt neglected. It's never about understanding *why* these things happened. Look at it like this: These situations were provided to you at a time that is now showing up as an opportunity to rise above them. To surrender to them. To embrace them with forgiveness, love, and compassion and move on to the next stage of your soul.

That's it. You can continue to hold onto them, you can put them in an archived box for later examination, or you can burn them. It's up to you.

Just Stand

It's a natural instinct to defend yourself. From the beginning of time, man has had to defend himself. Back then though, it was a life-threatening situation like being eaten by a dinosaur or saber-toothed tiger. Now the threats aren't really on your life per se, but on your ego. So that instinctual behavior of defense morphs into defense of the ego and becomes a learned behavior.

Why DO you feel the need to defend yourself anyway? Aren't you sure of who you are and what you stand for? Aren't you open to life's challenges as opportunities to grow, develop, and evolve? Can't you weather any storm with valor and courage?

No—you can't. Well you can, but you are programmed to do it differently—for now.

There a couple of ways you may be handling chaos or an attack on your ego. And remember, these are learned behaviors. See if any of these best describes you.

1. One choice: You recoil or retreat. You don't say anything because you just don't like confrontation.

2. Another option: You agree or go along with the attacker and do it their way just to keep the peace. It's easier to put up an invisible wall between you and the attacker.

3. A more aggressive option: You retaliate with an attack on the attacker. It puts a stop to their attack and you have shifted the focus to their shortcomings. Usually what happens is both of you get so off track you forgot what you were talking about in the first place.

4. A futile option: you stand there spewing defenses to prove the attacker wrong about how they feel about you. You continually defend yourself and try to change their judgment about the situation or who you are.

5. A peaceful, integrative option: you listen intently, take it all on your shoulders, and let the attacker's words affect how you think about yourself. You go deep into self-inquiry and evaluate if their words are true for you.

I would like to offer a more appropriate option: Just stand.

This is a very powerful and stoic option. Let the whirlwind of other people's judgments, perceptions, and words buzz around you. Do not be torn down by their words or actions against you. Do not let the chaos around you affect You. (Notice the capital Y… that's intentional.) I must caution you that when you do choose this option, your attacker may have no idea how to react and may choose to get even more aggressive. This is a challenge for you. It's OK… you can handle it.

You created this situation to purify your soul and live from a space of light, love, and divine guidance. You brought this person into your life to help you get past your ego and into your soul, especially if it is someone really close to you like your spouse, sibling, or parent. You created it!

When you can remember that you created it, it's so much easier to understand. You can embrace it and stand strong in it. Just stand.

Old Language

How do you know when you are evolving? Simple… start taking a breath or two or three or four between thought and reaction. How does this serve you?

Well, it gives you some time for internal reflection. For starters, you notice your physical body: where it hurts, where it's been neglected, and where it feels alive. You begin to notice how you relate differently to the same people in your life offering you the same challenges you have always had. What do I mean by this?

OK… follow me on this one. For example, let's say you have always had an issue with guilt. You feel guilty if you make more money than someone else, if you forget someone's birthday, if you work late instead of play with your kids, if you miss a date night with your partner… you name it. Everyone has feelings of guilt.

So you have this issue with guilt. And in the past, you have unconsciously allowed other people involved in these scenarios appeal to that guilt. "I wish I had the money to get a new outfit." "I remembered your birthday. You must be pretty busy to forget my birthday!" "You missed it! She pulled out her own tooth while you were at work again!" "I know I said we would this Friday… didn't you write it down?"

Sound familiar to anyone? You get the picture. These people know how to trigger your feelings of guilt. Not because they are mean or vindictive. YOU are the one allowing it to take you over; YOU are the one allowing it to bother you; YOU are the only one who can stop it.

Then one day (most likely after some work in this area of the body: yoga, self-inquiry, meditation, acceptance, and surrender) you let go of that guilt. You no longer truly experience guilt. You don't use the word in your vocabulary and you don't feel it; in fact, the feeling of guilt can't vibrate with you anymore because you have done the work to rise above it.

So then, these same people say the same things to you and you feel like you are watching a movie. You don't feel like you have to repel, justify, explain, walk away, or even discuss it. Their words just don't trigger you anymore. It's usually a jaw-dropping experience because you NOTICE the shift and they don't.

What do you think happens? They get mad, frustrated, and confused. Let me clarify: THEY don't get mad, frustrated, and confused—their ego does. Because they can't bring YOU to the level of the old, controlling language that once worked. They are very confused and aren't sure what language to use with you. Maybe they get more upset as time goes by and maybe you crack.

It's OK. Not to worry… you won't always crack. You're a spiritual being living a human experience, remember? Perfection is only in your effort. After some time and several replays of the same scenario, when you just stand there without reacting, listening to them use old language, they will get bored and move to someone else who IS vibrating on the same level as they are.

Alternatively, they could, if they were ready, notice what type of energy exchange was happening and they could take the opportunity to grow right alongside you, into that new vibrational frequency. But remember, you can't make them... don't even try.

Speak Your Truth

When you get to the throat chakra stage of your "house cleaning," you may find it challenging to speak your truth. You know you are standing on solid ground; you're not afraid. You can actually feel the flow of the Universe pushing you forward. All action up until now has been heart-centered and metabolized through conscious awareness.

So then why, when you go to speak it to others, is there still this huge lump in your throat? That's so annoying, isn't it? It's like, all this hard work and it's still stuck? REALLY?

It starts off small, to be honest. Think of a baby learning to talk, a child learning how to put a sentence together, or anyone studying a foreign language. It's new, so it takes practice. I have two suggestions for this process. Speak from a place of gratitude and compassion about what you notice to be true for the other person or situation. And then state your needs independently of what that person had done in this situation. I recommend doing this over and over and over again on small things.

So maybe your first new words are, "Honey, I really am grateful that you made dinner for me. And I just want to remind you that I really don't like fruit on my salad." You didn't say but or however in between those statements. They were completely independent of each other and both acceptable. You honored the other person for what they did for you and then you expressed your need.

Pretty simple, right?

The other suggestion I have is to start talking to yourself in the mirror. I know it seems silly, but it works. It's great practice for you to see yourself talking and how your facial expressions actually support or contradict what you are really trying to say. I have witnessed people saying, "Yes, I DO want to try yoga, I DO!" while they are shaking their head no. They have no idea what they are doing. So know what you are doing with your body that supports your words.

Now… once you have practiced this new you, it's time to try it on for the more emotionally-charged situations. This is where the lump seems to happen. Let's use some examples: you would like a raise, you want to stop working and go back to school, you want help around the house, you want to quit school and travel, you need some space, you have fallen out of love…

Gulp. Only you can't swallow… the lump is too big.

Use the principles from above. That's it! I promise they work! Find gratitude for everything that has led you to this decision you have made and then state your need. Make sure your body language is open and you are supporting your words with your gestures. It just gets easier from here. AND you empower others to do the same.

Stand in Your Truth

So now you are a professional at speaking your truth. You are speaking freely about the gratitude you feel. You are honoring others for the roles they play in your life. You are honoring yourself by asking for what you need. You are so connected to the Universe because it's handing you people and situations that completely support what you are stating! It's a miracle!

But now the trick is to stand in it all the time. Once you see how easy it is to speak your thoughts, the next stage of evolution is to stand in it all the time.

This can be challenging. If you are speaking about living your passion, but you are stuck in a job you hate… you're not living it. If you are telling people about how to eat whole and healthy foods and you stop and get fast food on the way home… you're not living it. If you teach yoga, but you expect too much of yourself, judge others, and experience separateness… you are not living it.

It's almost like your physical body and brain (which makes choices for you) have to catch up with your inner guidance system. You know it… you feel it… you express it when you live in slow motion or when you are alone. But man, when you have to live your truth all the time, in front of other people, it becomes a consistently conscious effort.

Let me remind you of something that is very important here… you are a spiritual being living a human experience. You are human and that's not an excuse… it just is what it is. As a human you were born to go through all this stuff that brings you back to your spiritual Self. So you are going to "get it wrong." Think of it as a misstep and then try again.

Eventually your body will support your inner spirit. One word of insight… surround yourself with the people who support you on this journey and

lovingly free the ones who don't. It makes it so much easier! The ones who don't support your new truth may watch from a distance or they may turn their backs. Either way, it's their choice, not yours.

Boundaries

In this lifetime, you can expect to experience love, loss, joy, pain, laughter, tears, and a whole myriad of emotions and experiences that make life worth living!

When you begin shifting and your thoughts, words, and deeds become different from the immediate circle you have created for yourself through friends and family, expect to be judged. Expect them to try and tear you down. THEY ARE NOT DOING THIS TO BE MEAN! They just don't know how to relate to you anymore! They want the old you back! This "new you" makes no sense to them and they can't deal with it anymore!

This is the only way they know how to relate their fear to you… they toss judgments at you. They want to try and keep you where you are. It's inevitable and it's a natural part of your growth. Now, some of these people will fall away from your life completely. But for the most part, if they are family and friends, they may stick around, but the relationship will change.

What can you do during this time of unsolicited judgment? Create some friendly, healthy boundaries for yourself. This isn't done to be vindictive or make them mad. It's done to protect you and your growth. You're like a little egg in an incubator. You need light and warmth and protection and sometimes, fighting off or defending yourself against judgment and perceptions just takes up too much energy.

So you set some boundaries—at least until you feel strong enough to really stand in your new truth. You limit the amount of face-to-face time. You steer phone conversations in the direction you want them to go. You articulate

exactly what it is that you need right now in order for you to continue to grow. You express gratitude for all they have done for you up until this point. You are clear, kind, and full of love for yourself, so you can't help but allow that to spill over into your relationship with them, but only because you have set boundaries.

You notice when they are unconsciously jabbing at you... provoking you to slip into old behaviors. You thank them silently for the chance to notice and move past it.

This will help you: Make a list of what you cannot tolerate any longer. Share this with the people who are important to you. They deserve a chance to work toward treating you this way. When they act out in a way that was acceptable to the old you and no longer acceptable for the new you, immediately remind them of your new boundaries.

Notice when you are getting caught up and letting the old you come back into the game. This happens, you know, especially with the ones you love the most or who have been around the longest. It's because they are speaking to you in a way that used to fire you up. If this happens again and again and again, your defenses may crack. It's OK... rebuild the boundary and try again.

It's exhausting to be honest, but only if you allow it to be exhausting. You choose what you allow into your sacred space. You choose how you will react. You choose when you will walk away or let them spiral out away from your boundary.

Tolerance

Think back to your life in grade school, middle school, high school, and maybe into college. Think of all the growth you have gone through. Do you ever think to yourself, "Geez, that seems like an entirely different lifetime!"

It's like watching the movie of your life from a distance... witnessing the choices you made, the mistakes you made, the lessons you learned, and the shift in what you tolerate and what you want along the way.

First off, when you do a "look back" on your life, it's important to look back in awe. It's imperative to let go of any regret, responsibility, or any negative emotions that are stuck there with regard to your choices, mistakes, and lessons learned. Bless the child you were and understand that every single choice you made along the way was necessary in order for you to get to where you are right now. Everything was divinely guided. I have to say that because sometimes people get stuck here and miss the point of the discussion I am about to move into.

When you experience a shift in what you tolerate and what you want, my personal belief is that it's your self-worth that has grown. Now, I am no expert on self-worth, but I can say this for sure: While you are growing up, your self-worth can either be supported or denied. And when you are young, you may not have a choice in the matter because your limited experience dictates your perception. Are you following me?

So let's say your self-worth was nurtured. With this, you probably make choices along the way that support who you are and what you stand for. You feel confident in your choices and you aren't going to worry about what other people think because you understand that you deserve nothing less. Still with me?

But let's say that from childhood through adolescence, your self-worth was not nurtured. In fact, it was knocked down. You did well, but it was only to prove that you were worthy of recognition. You settled for less because your thought was, "This is all I am worthy of." And to top it off, you spent time proving your worthiness and your deservedness of love for fear of losing what you had. Sound familiar to anyone?

Then one day you realize your true worth. You know that you are an angel with unique gifts. And sharing them is completely unrelated to any type of recognition, personal gain, or proof of your capabilities. What do you think happens when you take inventory of your life with regard to the choices you have made until now?

You start saying, "I thought that? I believed that? I tolerated that? NONE of that is who I am now! What the hell!? This life I have created is based on old beliefs about myself! Now what?"

You may feel stuck. You may start this contemplative journey back to all the choices you made based on your lack of self-worth. You may have a hard time figuring out how to move forward from here. But you can.

Redefine what you tolerate and share it with the people who are closest to you. Say out loud, "I am a new person and there are some new rules about how I will act and how I will be treated. I know this is going to be a journey for us all, so let's begin with cultivating patience as we move along this new road."

Sounds delicious, right? It can be… very much so. Just be prepared for guilt, resentment, and a backlash of, "I was good enough for you then. Why I am not good enough for you now?"

The only answer is… Because you're different.

Discern Truth

How do you discern truth for yourself? Do you know? What a huge question, right? Take it one step further, just to make it a little confusing, and now try and discern truth from illusion.

In order to do this effectively, because these are very objective concepts, I looked both words up in the dictionary.

Truth is has a variety of meanings, such as the state of being in accordance with a particular reality. It can also mean having fidelity to an original ideal. In a common archaic usage, it also meant constancy or sincerity in action or character.

Whoosh! That's heavy. Now let's look at illusion.

An illusion is a distortion of the senses, revealing how the brain normally organizes and interprets sensory stimulation. While illusions distort reality, they are generally shared by most people. Optical illusions are the most well-known and understood; however, illusions can be felt with the other senses. The emphasis on visual illusions occurs because vision often dominates

the other senses. Some illusions are based on general assumptions the brain makes during perception.

Even heavier, but makes technical sense, right?

So when you put these two definitions together, it would seem like Truth is your current state of reality and Illusion's job is actually to distort it. Now here's a truth you have been carrying around with you forever. For example, "I'm not good enough to be an artist," is no longer resonating with you. You no longer believe this truth. Did Illusion come in as the thought form: "You have a natural gift for painting and should get your work out there" and create distortion of your old, limiting truth? And now does "I have a natural gift for painting" become your new truth?

How many times do you think this has the potential to happen in your life— this shift of truth to illusion back to truth? Well, it could never happen for you, honestly. If you are stagnant in your beliefs and remain rigid in your thinking, this metaphysical phenomenon may never happen to you.

But on the other hand, if you are open and you are on a spiritual journey, it may happen constantly. In fact, now, with the world moving at the rapid pace that it is, truth and illusion sometimes become one. It can get very confusing, discerning truth from illusion—which is why it's important to pray, meditate, surround yourself with like-minded people, and create a sacred circle for yourself.

There is no right or wrong answer to what is truth. You must know for yourself and keep in mind that there are many expressions of the same truth.

One Truth, Many Expressions

You knew that last sentence had to lead to this Om, right? Exactly what does this mean? Simple… the best way I can describe this theory is to pull out the Yoga Sutras. Let's choose one randomly:

Sutra II:35 – *Ahimsa: In the presence of one firmly established in non-violence, all hostilities cease.*

How do you interpret this Sutra? Does this mean that when you are always acting from a place of peace, harmony, and non-violence that you will never experience violence? Does that mean that you just don't notice it? Or that you don't allow it?

How you do define non-violence? Do you mean that you don't kill anyone? You don't physically or verbally abuse another? You don't watch programs that promote violence? You don't kill bugs? You don't think harmful thoughts about others? About yourself?

The depth with which you answer this question is your own expression of your truth around the question and how you interpret it. Your perception of non-violence is very different than someone else's perception. Therefore, the same truth has many expressions.

Now start applying this to random statements you hear throughout your day. Start applying this to the judgments and opinions of other people. Start being open to the possibility that your truth has a different expression than those around you. Or, conversely, start being open to the possibility that your truth has a similar expressions to that of those around you and different from the truth you have been carrying around all these years.

Yup… fun stuff.

Inner Turmoil

Sometimes when you are going through a tough time, it's easier to suffer alone than it is to talk about your issues with someone else, isn't it? It's easier to say, "I'm FINE!" when people ask you how you are. (By the way, the acronym FINE is Frickin' Incapable of Normal Emotion—just saying.)

It may seem easier to do this, but I can tell you that in the long haul, it's much harder.

The people in your life who love and support you want to be there for you. They want to shower you with love and gratitude and prayer and strength. It's why we are here: to connect and support each other!

So why do you suffer alone when things get tough? Because someone told you not to burden other people with your problems. Because you are afraid of what people will think of you if you don't "have it all together." Because you wish it were different and talking about it just makes it more real for you.

These are all valid reasons for not opening up, but let me share something with you that may help you to get over that "I can do it all by myself" syndrome.

Holding things in creates dis-ease in the body. When you suffer alone and silently, your body feels that stress. It can't take it... although it is. On the outside, your body seems fine. You are functioning during your crisis, you are holding it together, and no one needs to know the difference.

But inside, your body is fighting itself. All the systems that keep you alive are working so damn hard just to get you through another day. Your immune system starts to suffer because it just can't keep up anymore. You have dreamless sleep and wake up with clenched teeth, which puts your spine out of alignment, giving you headaches you can't control without medication.

You have started on a downward spiral of killing yourself from the inside out just so you can buck up, prove that you have it all together, and meanwhile, pray that maybe things will change.

Guess what… things may change, but in the meantime, at this rate, you won't be around to see it. You'll be sick or dead.

Open up to the people around you who care about you and love you. Share your thoughts and say them out loud, if only one time to see how it feels. Cry, laugh, scream at the injustice, be afraid, get excited…experience every single emotion and let them flow through you as they were intended to do.

If it's change that needs to be made on your part, do it as soon as you can. There is a fine line between releasing it and moving on and continuing to beat a dead horse, if you know what I mean. Use your energy wisely… you are only issued one physical body and there are no refunds, returns, or exchanges.

Freedom

When I see this word, I feel like jumping high into the air, naked, on the beach at sunset.

What does freedom mean to *you*?

I looked it up in the dictionary and it has so many meanings:

The state of being free rather than under physical restraint; exemption from external control; release from ties and obligations; the ease of movement; and my favorite: *the power to exercise choice and make decisions without constraint from within or without.*

Doesn't that just make you want to get up and jump and say, "WOO-HOO!"

What would freedom look like to you? Not sure?

Ask yourself: Are you feeling restraints anywhere in your life? Maybe they aren't necessarily physical restraints, but they are restraints nonetheless. Where do you feel it in your body when you consider those restraints?

What about your ties and obligations? We all have obligations and responsibilities in life, but how much do you let them control your life and make decisions for you? All the time? Some of the time? Never? Examine just how much if you are feeling less than free in this area of your life. If your obligations are running your life, it's time to make a change.

The ease of movement... oh, holy heck! YOGA! Right!!! The ease of movement is found in the lovely practice of yoga. And the beauty is you can meet yourself where you are right now. No need to push yourself, expect anything, or commit to more than your body can handle; just show up with an ease of movement.

And then my personal favorite... the power to exercise choice and make decisions without constraint from within or without. The key here, for me, is the "make decisions without constraint from within..." Forget about the "without." Any constraint you perceive from the outside is a manifestation of your own mind. But this "from within" is so important.

YOU create your own constraints... YOU DO! No one else! So guess what? Your freedom or lack of freedom is up to you... and you alone. You get to make the decision that you can feel freedom right now... yes, right now... because you are the only one who thinks or perceives it to be any different. Yippee! Go for it... JUMP!

Giving Within Your Own Boundaries

How many of you feel spent at the end of the day? You actually hear yourself saying, "I cannot give one more inch of myself!" I have been known to say that to my very perplexed little girls… once or twice.

But really, how much energy, if you could measure it for yourself, do you expend each day? Would you say that you have any in reserve when you finally fall into bed at night? Or are you tapping into your reserves just to get through your day?

For most of you, you are tapping into your reserves each and every day. And I'm talking about the reserves on all levels of your being…. physically, emotionally, mentally, and spiritually. Every square inch of our being is being utilized to get through your days.

How do you think that is serving you? How is it serving your family, friends, and coworkers? I know you know the answer. How do you make a shift?

You stop and set some new boundaries. Do you think that anyone in your life (your boss, your spouse, your children) is going to make new boundaries for you so you can feel better? They are not.

You have to do this for yourself. And it's important because truly you are the only one who knows where to set that line up for your optimal health and well-being.

Try this… break your day up into three-hour increments. Then make a list of all the people to whom you give during your day. Quick sidebar question: Are you on that list anywhere? If you are not, you need to be, so just put yourself on there and can get in the lineup.

Now, on another sheet of paper, write out an overview of what you do daily and weekly. Just an overview—no need for full-on details.

Now sit back and look at what you are currently doing. It's too much, right? Look to see what's a necessity and find a spot for it on your new three-hour increment sheet. Can you change the way you are doing things so there isn't so much time wasted? Can you give responsibility away and ask for help with some of these things? And then put yourself in there somewhere. And make sure it's not you cleaning house, doing the bills, or helping with homework. Make sure it's meditating, doing yoga, sitting in the tub, or doing nothing.

When It's Over

How do you know when a relationship, job or circumstance is over—when you have just had enough and been pushed to your absolute limit for the very last time? You know. Through tears, sadness, deep sorrow, and a broken heart, your courage stands up and says, "That is enough! It's over. My heart and soul cannot continue to compromise any longer!"

And you know because the *why* doesn't matter. The *what will people think* doesn't matter. The *what will happen if* doesn't matter. Nothing matters. Your heart has watched the same movie too many times and it wants new meaning. It is yearning to play, to have fun, to dance, to sing, and to enjoy life, and it cannot in its current state of survival.

If you can remember that your life is in a constant state of ebb and flow, then you can surrender to the inevitability of endings. Endings of relationships and careers, relocation of your current home...you name it, everything changes.

How do you know when it's over and it's time for a change? When the web of stories are too intricate to unravel. When "I'm sorry" doesn't mean anything. When you get tired of hearing yourself say the same things over and over

again, knowing that the outcome will be exactly the same. When you know that when you speak your truth, this is the last time you "complain."

How do you know when it's over? When you can't bear to look into that person's eyes anymore. When their words and actions that used to trigger you just don't bother you anymore. When you would rather be alone in a huge house than together in a small room. When you go to work and feel heavy and exhausted before you even get there. When your stomach hurts every single minute of every single day?

But most of all you know it's over when you recognize Self Love. When you know that in your heart of hearts, you are more than what you are going through. When the love you have finally found for yourself is stronger than any love or any pain that you could feel for anyone or anything.

This is when you know. And your ego mind has nothing to do with it. In fact, your ego is the one who has kept you here all along, rooted in fear. The ego wanted things to stay the same because that's predictable. All along your heart knew better, but you just weren't ready to listen.

Keep in mind that each person and each situation is different and unique. Only YOU know when your heart is ready to jump out of your chest, ablaze in courage and righteousness. You hear a voice that says, "It's time." No one can tell you when it's over. No one can help you decide. No one can judge your decision either. They aren't living your life, sleeping in your bed, "walking in your shoes". They don't know any of the anguish or the hurt you have endured. They haven't watched the same movie over and over again, wondering when the channel is going to change.

How will you know when it's over? You just know that it's got to be better than the movie you are watching right now. You will know for sure when you slowly exhale, knowing that everything will be okay in time.

Embrace Your Power

Ask yourself what will it take for YOU to embrace your amazing power? You were born with a gift—something that is uniquely your own. Maybe along your path you forgot you had this power. Maybe people and circumstances brought you to an inappropriate belief that you were less than someone who could love life, laugh from your gut, share love freely, experience inner peace, and enjoy overwhelming abundance and joy in the world around you.

If you aren't experiencing that right now, you forgot who you are. You have been snagged by the world ego telling you something less than what your heart knows to be true.

Let me ask you a question… in your most powerful moments, how do you see yourself? Do you envision climbing a huge mountain? Can you feel yourself surfing the waves? Are you silent in the midst of amazingly tall trees?

Do you express unconditional love for all that you were, gratitude for who you are, and wonderment about who you are becoming? Do you understand and embrace the fact that every step of your journey was important in the natural progression of your life? Do you let go when it's time and move on gracefully and compassionately?

Can you look at yourself in the mirror and know that you are giving all that you can to yourself first and then sharing your abundance with others? Do you know who your most amazing friends are and share a love that is more powerful than any fear, illusion, or hurt?

Do you fall silent in the breath of miracles like a bird sitting in a tree, the leaves falling, flowers blooming, and your children laughing? Can you rise

above the pettiness and unpredictable life that is whirling around you?

For me, my power was unrecognizable until I spent considerable time on my mat. It took me years of physical exploration, self-inquiry, and emotional upheaval before I knew that I held this amazing power. In fact, to be honest, I didn't know I actually owned this power until I decided to leave my marriage. It wasn't until then that I knew I had the courage to do anything in the name of self-love.

Self-love is where you hold your power. It isn't about the power you hold over another, the power you have to change someone's mind, the power you have to make money, or the power you exude to control any outcome in your life. Power comes with self-love. It comes with loving yourself so much that you know that whatever decision you make—you are backed up by the Universe. It comes with loving yourself so much that you know when it's time to change direction. The self-love spills over into every area of your life and you recognize, finally, that you have the power to make life happen— that there is light and beauty all around you all the time.

You just never noticed it before, but there it is… YOU. The most radiant, powerful YOU. Don't ya just love you?

Falling Into Your Truth

Do you believe that people change? I do. In fact, the reality is that we are always evolving. To be clear, we are given daily opportunities to evolve. Whether or not we choose to take those opportunities and use them for the evolution of our soul is another matter.

Every day, the truth about what you believe about life and how it's showing up for you is challenged. You are offered circumstances every day not to "learn a lesson," but to instead rearrange your life according to your evolving truth and what you believe about yourself.

During this time of "monumental shifts," every area of your thinking is challenged. What you think about the world around you, about love, about finances, about spiritual connection, and about your ability to navigate from a soul perspective shifts.

While you are busy walking this very thin line, balancing between truth and illusion, your life may seem chaotic. It may seem like you are witnessing circumstances that represent your truth and your illusion. "Random circumstances" happen "to" you, displaying the unsupportive stance of your blurred way of thinking.

Because of this, you become even more confused about your own truth and illusion. You know you feel a shift within you, but you feel a little immobilized about how to truly live it. It's a little foreign to you.

Keep in mind that all the while, your soul is screaming at you through dreams, through unconscious thoughts, through angels that show up as "coincidental meetings," that THIS IS IT! The time is NOW! You KNOW your truth and all you have to do is believe in yourself.

The challenging part of this huge step toward growth is that you have never been here before. The ground beneath your new truth seems so far away... what if you fall? It's all so confusing, but it's only confusing because YOU keep vacillating between the old and the new versions of you. YOU are not accepting who you are becoming—most likely out of fear.

Remember that you are here to grow, evolve, and develop. You are here to bring yourself to a point in your life where you realize that Universal support is part of your everyday thinking. You know it, you feel it, you embody it, and you are able to live your life from a place of service and connectedness.

In order to live the life you dream of, and at some points of your day "feel" to be true and real, at some point you are going to have to fall into the new paradigm of what you believe to be true. You are going to have to fall off that tightrope and trust that the Universal net is going to catch you. You can do this without even looking down.

Affirmations & Postures

You can be a goal-setting, intentional individual, but remember that there is something bigger than all of us. Let's honor that and ask for guidance… every single day.

Allow your feelings to flow through you so you can move that energy out

Make sacred time for your thoughts, every day. If you don't, you'll notice repeat after repeat after repeat. If you do, your life will unfold according to the map of your soul… because you let it breathe.

You have a choice about what you want to do with "your stories". You can continue to hold onto them, you can put them in an archived box for later examination, or you can burn them. It's up to you.

When you can remember that you created any and all situations in your life for your evolution, it's so much easier to understand. You can embrace it and stand strong in it. Just stand.

You have to understand the darkness to really feel gratitude for the light.

The people who don't support your new truth may watch from a distance or they may turn their backs. Either way, it's their choice, not yours.

Anahata

Camel

Bridge

Cobra

Shoulderstand

Plough

Butterfly

Fish

Chapter 6
On Illusion versus Intuition
Third Eye Chakra: Ajna

What Do You Envision?

That's such a huge question, isn't it? It can cover so much territory! The answer can be very broad, like "I want peace on Earth" or super specific, like "I want to have a job that allows me the time and money to support leisurely travel."

There are a couple of things here that are interesting to me. So why don't you experience peace on Earth or a job that offers you complete financial freedom? Because the question is a trick question. To answer it, you would say, "I want," which actually confirms lack. And when you state to the Universe, "I want," you are actually saying,

"I don't have that, please give me more of not having that!"

Now change the question a wee bit to "What Do You Envision?"

A-ha! Now you can say, "I see peace on Earth," or "I love my current job and it will be so nice when I work a more flexible schedule and I am paid enough money to travel the globe." The words become more powerful, wouldn't you agree?

But the bigger question, beyond how you answer a question like, "What do you want?" is: *How many of you really know what you want? What do you envision for yourself with regard to your relationships, your career, your health, your lifestyle, your environment, your finances?*

When was the last time you actually answered a question like that—seriously sat down and answered that question from a place of intentional manifestation?

This is the single most important thing you can do for yourself right now. Why? Because your answers steer your life. Your answers to these questions will create your reality. You can't escape your true thoughts because they show up as your life.

Every thought you have becomes a reality—every single one, every single time. What do you want? What do your relationships look like? How do you approach the energy of money? How do you feel in your home? In your current job? Answer those questions honestly and then really look at your current situation in those areas. Are they in alignment with how you feel right now?

Maybe not… because your reality right NOW is based on PAST thoughts. What's your thought right NOW? Create it. YOU have the power to create your life EXACTLY as you intend. Be clear and envision, then act.

What Are You Afraid Of?

Now that you have clarified what you want in this lifetime, ask yourself, "What am I afraid of?" Because if you aren't experiencing what you envision right now, the only thing keeping you from it is fear. (Or the illusion that you already don't "have" it…)

Fear—that's what keeps you suffering. But fear of what?

Only you can answer that question. Your first reaction to this statement is to deny that it's fear and instead blame you're not "having" something on someone else, the economy, your finances, your situation, or any number of reasons that are outside yourself. But the truth of the matter is that YOUR fear(s) and beliefs keep you from what you want. It's as simple as that.

So what are you afraid of? Getting hurt? Losing everything? Failing miserably? Being alone? People judging you? Not being accepted? Making the wrong decision? Everyone finding out who you REALLY are? What is it? You've GOT to recognize what you are afraid of, otherwise you will keep spinning in this "I want" whirlwind forever!

What's funny is if you sit down and really meditate on what you're afraid of, a lot of the time it's very silly. And by silly I mean, when you state your fear, it makes no sense. Most of the time, fears are based on illusion. They are based on past experiences, other people's fears, or limiting beliefs about your true capability. Fears are irrational.

But fears have the power to plague you and stop you every single time! Because they are swirling around in your mind, your mind has a way of making a mountain out of a molehill! Your ego, which controls the mind, puts these fears in front of you so you continually remain in your comfort zone, where it's safe and secure and predictable. But that's no place to live if you envision more for yourself or for this world.

Pinpoint those fears… face them… jump into them… roll around in them… affirm they are not yours or that they do not pertain to you. Understand that the soul has no fear! Recognize that your fears are stopping you and you are the only person who can eradicate them once and for all.
NOW is the time… YOU are being called to give your gift. How dare you keep your gift to yourself based on fear! Get in there and then get out there. Dig deep, people… it's where all the light lives. And then get out there and shine!

Totally Exposed

I don't know if you all know this, but the world is moving faster. Some call it the technological age, but I like to believe it's much bigger than that. Technology is only a consequence of the reality of what is happening on a Universal level. We have no control over it. It is what it is.

Time is moving quicker, we take in more information in one day than people 100 years ago received in their entire lifetime, the Earth is spinning faster, our thoughts become things instantly, and we have the opportunity to systematically strip away our dense layers because of the speed of life.

I visualize it like this… we're part of this crazy, undeniable whirlwind and we have a choice. We can spin along with it and allow the layers to be peeled back, offering us a chance to be, do, and contribute what we were meant to in this lifetime. Or we can fight against it, standing stiff as a board, back hunched over, clenching our fists like an angry child, holding steady against the whirlwind, clinging to old patterns, beliefs, and thoughts, unwilling to expose ourselves to what is true.

How does it feel to be totally exposed? Define it for yourself. Is it scary, un-comfortable, painful, embarrassing, or forbidden? Can you define it as free-ing, comfortable, easy, enlightening, and almost electric?

It can be all of those things. If you are the angry child trying to control the whirlwind around you, ask yourself why are you avoiding the inevitable? Why are you fighting the wind? Ask yourself what you are hiding that you don't want others to know about. What would happen if they found out what you are hiding? Would it be scary or freeing?

Visualize yourself being free from the things that keep you from being totally exposed. What would that look like? How light could you feel? How would you express yourself? How much energy could you free from your thoughts? How close would you be to the Divine Source?

Now ask yourself how you can take that first step. The road to evolution is first involution, embracing what holds you back, owning it, loving it, and then releasing it.

Are you in?

The Real World

I seriously love, love, love listening to my daughters talk about life. They are little spirits—so conscious and awake! I am extremely blessed to witness their

reality. They create with no boundaries, act from their truth, tell it like it is, and dream with no limits. Every day they inspire me to think outside the box.

The other day we were talking about what they wanted to be when they grew up. Currently, they are both demonstrating an authentic drive to be little entrepreneurs. Isabella had a great idea to build a four-story building that was a fashion-spa-makeover palace for you and your pet. I encouraged her to visualize it and draw it so she could make her dream a reality one day. And I plan on keeping the drawing for when she begins her journey into the "real world."

What were your dreams as a kid? What did you want to do? Do you remember? I wanted to be a cowgirl and a concert pianist and ironically, a journalist.

Presently, I own a cowboy hat, I am learning to play "Hot Cross Buns" with Ava, and I'm a journalist, all right!

After you remind yourself about your childhood dreams, ask yourself, are you witnessing any of them right now? If not, what got you off track? When did you get off track? Maybe your dreams are just on hold… but for how long? Have you put a timeline on the hold? How long will you choose to live in the "real world" that has been defined by other people?

Even when I say those words, I cringe. Maybe because I have seen too many people fall prey to the "real world" and then never leave it. They let go of the soul's intention of seeking their highest potential and instead they fulfill the roles they have been assigned. They become dense and weighed down. They become of the world and not in it. They let other people drown their inner voice of connection, dreams, and imagination with reason, logic, and "reality."

I'm sorry, but that stinks. Can you imagine how amazing this world would be if more and more people listened to their hearts and remembered what they LOVE about this life?

If you ever say to yourself, "How did I get here?" know that you have made decisions based on today's "realities" and not tomorrow's dreams. You lost sight of YOU. And if you ever imagine something better for yourself, you are imagining it because your heart knows it is so.

The Diving Board

I was sitting with a friend of mine over the weekend— she was the inspiration for this week's Om. She came to me and said something like this, "You know, I remember when I was a kid and I had to take swimming lessons. And I remember standing on the edge of the diving board, with everyone waiting for me, and I was terrified to jump. Eventually my teacher pushed me straight off the edge and into the water. I hated it."

I had a similar experience, so I could feel her story completely.

And then we started discussing how that can be such a metaphor for life and how we approach it.

So let me ask you: How many times are you faced with a decision about your path? A choice about which road to take? A push to do what comes next in your life? As you know, you make thousands of decisions each day. However, in this case, I'm talking about the bigger decisions. The decisions that are monumental and pivotal in your life. The ones that could change the direction of your life completely. Those decisions usually take time to percolate and you usually imagine all the various outcomes before you make those decisions, right?

A couple of things come to mind for me with this visualization, so I want to explore both of them.

The first is this: You can imagine and visualize every "outcome" to your decisions and still have no clue what will really happen. Really, who are you to KNOW what any outcome of your decisions will be? You have no clue. You can visualize and think it into being… you know that thoughts create your reality. However, when it's decision-making time, it's helpful to be open to the greater grace and instead allow the Universe to unfold as it was meant to, not unfold by the limits of your own thinking. Make sense?

Now consider a decision that is so monumental that it triggers past situations that have been painful or scary. What do you do then? Do you just sit with it? Kind of like hanging at the edge of the diving board? You unconsciously put yourself in this place where you figure that the Universe will decide the outcome for you. That is much easier than making the decision yourself. This way, you can let go of the responsibility.

It is much easier to just let things unfold as they should, right? And then what happens? The Universe finally pushes you off the proverbial diving board into your next decision, which can turn out just fine, but sometimes that can be sort of, dare I suggest, the wimpy way to go.

There is an in-between. Graceful intentions, yes. But more than that: Make decisions for yourself without attachment to any outcome. Have faith that the decisions you make will lead you to your next stage of evolution. Visualize possible outcomes for yourself, but remain open to what the Universe wants for you, too… without understanding it or even submitting to it.

Let go of fear as you jump off the diving board into the water below, nose plugged and eyes squeezed tight. Let it happen. Know that you are safe, that you will emerge - maybe after hitting the bottom - and exhale completely.

What If?

I have a close friend who lives in the world of "what if." What if you don't make it? What if you lose money? What if you hurt yourself? What if you don't get the job? What if, what if, what if… it drives me insane!

Are you a "what if" kind of person? Don't be embarrassed to admit it… it's okay. Most people are. But, it's comforting to know that if you are a "what if" person, you aren't that way by nature.

"What if" comes issued with the ego. "What if" comes from outside perceptions and other people's fears. "What if" comes in when OTHER PEOPLE are scared and they PROJECT their fears onto you.

The funny thing is that none of us can ever know or even begin to fathom "what if." I mean, we can imagine "what if" to any scenario we can think of... however, our realm of ideas is so limited. The "what ifs" are for those individuals who are fearful of moving forward for one reason or another. Those people are afraid of seeing their true greatness for fear of failure. The "what ifs" are reserved for those people who have lost sight of the greater power that guides us each day... something beyond what our own eyes can see.

Let's turn this "what if" around.

What if you found love greater than you can imagine for yourself? What if you let go and life handed you everything you ever dreamed of? What if you could feel joy every single minute of every single day? What if you could travel the world with your kids, make millions on your books, donate to several charities of your choice, know true love, surround yourself with people who inspire you, and experience the hand of God in everything you did?

What if?

Remember, they're YOUR thoughts, your decisions, your "what ifs." Personally, I like to DREAM BIG... it's never failed me before.

Emptiness

This is such an interesting word when you think about it. Empty what? Stomach, heart, mind, space, life... empty what?

When you feel emptiness, what is your natural tendency? To fill up that emptiness, right?

Think about it. You have an empty wall at home... hang a picture! Your glass is empty... fill it up! Your stomach rumbles... eat! You're talking to someone and there is silence all of a sudden... say something! You have some quiet

time at home… turn on the television! You fall out of love or end a relationship and your heart is empty… find someone new!

Hurry… fill it up!

Why do you feel the need to fill up emptiness? What are you scared of? Feeling something like pain or sadness? Are you afraid of being alone or worse yet, lonely? You can be lonely in a room full of people! You can be lonely in a long term relationship. It's ok to be alone…there is a difference you know.

Emptiness is a good thing! It's where wonder grows! It's where you actually feel your feelings. It's where divine inspiration meets manifestation! It's where you find yourself alone and vulnerable. It's where you can explore your true nature and actually feel energy moving through you.

This is why yogis detox. It's not to prove anything, get thin or have amazing physical bodies. It's to consciously access the subtle body. It's to feel vibrational energy move through them. It's to connect to the Universal power that is accessible to every single spiritual being walking this planet.

Energy has a hard time moving in dense situations or bodies. In fact, energy gets stuck in most people because they are dense. If you will, try to think of density in terms of physical, mental *and* emotional.

It's easy to visualize a "full" or "dense" person with regard to physical weight. But what about someone's mental state? Or someone's emotional state? Is that you?

If so, empty yourself already. And stay empty for a little while. Be okay with hunger pangs. Be okay with grief. Be okay with indecision. Be okay with being alone and sitting with your fears. Be okay with whatever feeling is passing through your emptiness. It's put there for you to feel it. You have just gotten used to being full and never noticed. It needs to move in order to do its work and it needs emptiness to do that.

Dreams

What are your dreams? Your deepest, most lovable dreams? About life? About love? About the world? What... are... your... dreams?

Do you know? When was the last time someone asked you that question? When was the last time you offered yourself some time to answer that question? Too long to remember?

I see it happen all too often. As you "grow up," you compromise your dreams for many reasons. One reason you may put your dreams on hold is because life hands you cards that don't seem to hold those dreams anywhere. At least, you can't see it, so you bag it.

Maybe you dreamed of being a traveling journalist. You dreamed of traveling the world and documenting your travels. And then, guess what? You had some kids, moved to suburbia, got wrapped up in their interests and dreams and forgot about your own.

Sound familiar?

Another reason your dreams get put off is because you allow other people to rain on your parade. You let other people talk you out of what you want to do based on their beliefs, insecurities, and judgments about your dreams. This happens when you have lack of commitment. You don't need all the facts, but THEY think you do. This is typical for anyone who breaks free from the "tribe." So you put it off until you can play it a bit safer.

Sound familiar?

And lastly, you put off your dreams because of fear. Fear of failing, of looking like a fool, of losing everything, of not making it, of having to live up to a higher standard... of being abnormal!

Sound familiar?

But you know what? If you put off your dreams, you are robbing the world of your natural talent. You are robbing the world of the God-like qualities that you came here to share. No one is like you. No one has the same gift as you. No one on this planet can walk your walk or talk your talk. Not one person. And if you don't share it... no one will ever experience your gift...ever.

Let your dreams become larger than your fears. Take a look at your fears. Follow them to their source and know they are nothing but something YOU made up in your mind. Or most likely, they are the fears of your parents, siblings, friends, or acquaintances. They are not your fears at all.

Let your dreams become larger than your fears. It will make the world a much better place.

The Spiritual Train

So you're on this spiritual train ride, right? You are waking up to who you were meant to be! How exciting! For a while, it's such a fun ride! It seems as if all the people in your life who are close to you are very happy and excited, too. They are on the train ride with you and life is just chugging along!

You begin living in the flow... for real! People who are in alignment with your new truth are entering your circle of awareness! You begin learning new things about the world around you. You adapt new ideas and practices that are alive and mean something to you. You feel this new vibrational energy and you just know this was meant to be your next stage of evolution.

Then there is a nagging feeling. It shows up in the form of someone close to you. Your spouse, your mother, father, sibling, or close friend is not understanding or subscribing to where you are headed.

They have a general sense of fear about where your train (you) is headed. It's unfamiliar ... there is no reason for it, really... but they are fearful. They treat you as they always have , but now their words are different somehow.

It's usually an unconscious provoking game. They aren't intending to hurt you or consciously bring you down off this train, but they speak old language that used to keep you off the train of evolution. They want to keep you right where you are... it's safe for *them*.

They are learning from you and they just don't want to share, really. I mean, if they share you, they may lose you. They may not be as important to you as they once were. They are riddled with fear about what is going to happen next.

For a while you may fall into this trap. It's only natural. You love them. You want them on your fun train ride. So you step off for a moment or two, re-assuring them that all is well. You are still the same person you have always been. You will always love them and everything is just fine.

You get back on the train with them in tow. They are a little reluctant to get on, but they do out of curiosity and out of fear. The ride is a little different this time. They aren't as interested in your train ride. In fact, they talk down about your new ideas, thoughts, and friends. Not only that, but they begin to step away from the support they once gave you and actually begin going in the complete opposite direction.

Eventually they get off at the next stop or jump off the train. What do you do?

I can tell you what I did. I jumped off and tried again and again and again. Want to know what I learned? You can't make anyone get on a train ride with you. They have to want to get on all on their own. Technically, they have to buy their own ticket.

By you continually trying to convince your loved ones that this new path of growth is great for both of you, and it will yield so many benefits for you and your family, you expend energy that is wasted on justification when it could be put to better use.

No matter how close you are to someone... they have to take their own spiritual train ride at their own pace. You can't make them want it, understand it, subscribe to it, live it, or be passionate about it. They have their own journey.

It's hard to let someone you love get off your train without a fight. But sometimes you have to in order to let them grow and evolve. Asking them to grow at your pace is selfish and doesn't help anyone.

So let go gracefully, lovingly, and compassionately. Everyone has their own journey and sometimes, the people you think are meant to be there by your side forever were just important teachers for a short amount of time.
You must recognize when it's time to let go and know, beyond all shadow of a doubt, that every individual you meet will get on their own train in their own time. Who knows, maybe you will be on the same train at some random stop?

You will be okay and so will they.

Scared of the Truth

Have you ever known what your next stage of evolution was but were afraid to move toward it because you knew that everything you believed about yourself was going to shift? That this shift meant that you would potentially lose everything you defined as safe, secure, and familiar.

It happens. When you begin a spiritual journey, the first few steps can be scary, even painful. You begin moving toward a new definition of what you believe to be true. And it may be completely opposite of what you have lived by in the past, so the road could be really dark and lonely. You may even turn back a few times just to be sure that you are on the right path. You are leaving familiarity, safety, and security for a perceived idea that this is the road of growth and expansion for you.

From a physical standpoint... when you commit to this movement, you are pulled in two directions. One is familiar and one is not. You may experience actual pain in the body manifesting itself as tight muscles, upset stomach, or constricted breathing.

From an energetic standpoint, your chakras are on fire! They are spinning and moving and connecting with each other! It's an exciting time! But it's also a time of mixed emotions, confusion, and isolation. You WILL be judged by others. You WILL be challenged to PROVE yourself. You WILL be tested on your resolve and commitment.

Don't be afraid. You know the truth. You feel it in your heart, your gut, and your bones. You dream about it. You visualize it. You breathe it in and out. Sometimes it's so clear, you actually see it as if it has already manifested.

That road to truth takes courage. I mean, really… most people hang onto familiarity and comfort. It's easier. But hanging onto familiarity kills the spirit. From what I have witnessed, when you choose familiarity over the fear of the unknown, you wind up in the same boat year after year after year. You create suffering for yourself because you know you have to move, but you can't… you're afraid.

Pay attention to your dreams. Pay attention to your external influences. Pay attention to the signs moving you in a new direction. You know… there may just be more love, excitement, joy, and authenticity on the other side. Don't be afraid. You are supported and you are loved.

Dying While Living

This is an interesting one for me to write. It was only just yesterday when I experienced what this really meant. It can potentially create quite a powerful shift if you are open to it.

When you begin moving toward your new life, your spiritual alive-ness, and your liberation from the past…your old life will begin shifting.

Think about an earthquake. The plates of the earth actually shift. That's what your life begins to feel like. Old friends may stop communicating with

you, your job may change, your marriage may end, you may have to move… things will change and it will most likely happen very rapidly.

The tendency is to grasp at the old, right? To keep a piece of it like a security blanket, just so you know that everything is going to be OK. But that can't happen. You can't take it with you. You have to let it go and let it go completely.

There are two ways to look at the phrase "dying while living." You have two choices as I see it:

You can choose to stay where you are… familiarity, perceived security and comfort, and you can allow your soul to die. You can allow your soul to quiet down so much that it just stops trying. You can go back to the slumber of your former life. This is a right that you have.

Now, I must caution you about this choice. If you do this, your soul will never, ever completely go back to sleep. You will continually feel the pulls from your heart. It will haunt you like the hounds of heaven (thanks, Michael Beckwith) until you honor it in some way. You will suffer because your soul knows better than anyone, even you, what is best for you. This is just a word of caution, and just my opinion—you can take it or leave it.

The other choice is allowing the ego take a backseat and let the soul guide your life. This is a powerful shift, because on many levels, if you choose to lead with your heart and your soul, you will feel the ego dying. You will feel it in every square inch of your body. You will most likely cry, scream, and physically fight it because that is the ego trying so damn hard to hold on. But your heart is stronger…it knows. It's supporting you because you allowed it to. You trusted it to carry you in times of perceived trouble.

Once the crying and physical turmoil stops, you are left with a vibrating energy that has to actually leave the body. You must stop and honor that activity.

Remember, you are energy. If you hold onto the energy of the ego dying, it will never die. It will continue to get in when it can and talk over the soul. Let the energy die off so you can become new and whole in this lifetime—guided only by your heart.

Either way is scary, but only one choice provides spiritual freedom.

Jump On… the Ride Will Stop Eventually

Nothing is permanent…nothing. Everything changes…it's a natural progression. There is no way anything could stay the same forever… it would go against the laws of the Universe.

So why do we fight it? Why do we fight and resist change? Why do we cling to what was when everything in the Universe is shifting so it can move to what is? Why? It's silly that we put this undue stress upon ourselves. We are the only species that does this, by the way.

Look at the chaos in your life like that ride at the amusement park that looks like an octopus—the one that goes around and around really fast and it flies up and down and sometimes the cart you are in randomly goes upside down. Do you know the one I am talking about? Okay, I HATE that ride. I think about it and my stomach hurts.

Equate that ride to your life when you are experiencing change or perceived chaos.

In order to change, transform or evolve, you have to get on that ride. You have to get on with love and appreciation and hang on tight. Hang on tight to your new perceptions, beliefs, and ideas about the world around you as you spin and drop and flip because that is what change feels like.

If you can hold onto your new ideas, you will be just fine when the ride finally stops—a little disoriented, a little disheveled, and maybe a bit turned around, but just fine.

And the ride will stop as will your turmoil. Remember nothing is permanent… not even turmoil. You can choose to hold onto turmoil for your entire life or you can get on and ride it out with truth in hand, just waiting for it to stop.

I promise… it will stop and on the other side will be light, love, and peace like you have never known. You just have to trust.

An Awakening

I love that word…awakening. What does it mean, really? Awakening to what? Reality? Truth? Illusion? Awakening to what?

Let's keep it simple… awakening to consciousness. It's that easy: an awakening to consciousness, an awakening to the fact that you are a pure spirit walking this planet and you have a birthright to be joyful all the time, an awakening to the fact that choices you have made in the past no longer matter, an awakening to the fact that you are interconnected to all that is and that there is no separation, an awakening to the fact that every person and circumstance in your life is for your own personal growth.

It's ALL an awakening! Once you get that first feeling of actually being ALIVE on this planet… awakening from your deep and intoxicating sleep… you can't help but notice so much more about the world around you. It's bigger and smaller all at the same time.

I will be honest. Awakening to the world around you can be daunting at first. All of a sudden, you become the observer of your life. You notice the people and circumstances around you in such a different light. You witness yourself acting out in ways that no longer serve you. You hear yourself talk, you notice your thoughts, and you start asking yourself where those thoughts and words actually came from. Are they coming from the soul or the ego?

Waking up to the world and to your Self is an amazing journey. Not everyone gets there in this lifetime. But once you get there, you can never go back to sleep… not ever. Your soul will always yearn to be heard and expressed.

What happens when you awaken? You shift and everything around you shifts, too. But it's not really shifting... your perception is shifting. You recognize your amazing human potential and you live it fully as often as you can. You see the beauty in others and you bestow gratitude on them. You forgive your own shortcomings so you are more open to forgiving others.

An awakening can happen over a lengthy period of time or it can happen in one moment. It all depends on how open you are to receiving and recognizing it. Your soul is begging to be heard... wake up already and listen.

The Middle of the Street

Ever have to make a huge life decision? Like whether or not to leave your job? Move to another state? Start a career based on your passion? Close your business? Leave your marriage? Tell someone the truth about something you have been lying about all along?

Just reading those examples can cause anyone's stomach to flip and heart to race, am I right?

It's kind of like standing in the middle of the road, not knowing which side of the street to get to for safety. You KNOW you have to move; you're in the middle of the street! If you don't move, you're going to get hit by a car and then poof! The decision will be made for you. You'll be dead, so it won't matter. (Or hurt badly, anyway.)

So, I ask you... if standing in the middle of the street causes you to feel physical stress, worry, fear, and general unrest... why do you continue to stand there? Why can't you pick a side of the street? What's the problem?

Not sure which side is going to yield the "right" space, answers, or circumstances for you? Guess what... you will never know until you GET OUT OF THE MIDDLE OF THE STREET ALREADY!

You have to let go of the outcome, let go of your choice being "right" or "wrong," and just MOVE! You have no control either way you go... YOU don't know what will happen. But you do know what will happen if you stay where you are. You will get smashed.

If you feel like you are in the middle of the road, needing to make a choice, do it now. The world is waiting...ready to offer you all that you need to fulfill your soul's purpose. You just have to let go of the ego, gain strength and courage, and move.

Pick a side, any side. But follow your heart and know what quality you need to get there. Use it... it's in you waiting to be birthed.

The Crystal Ball

Wouldn't it be nice to look into a crystal ball and actually SEE your future? You would know exactly what decisions to make in order to get to your predetermined future. You would know exactly what was going to happen and when! You wouldn't have anything to worry about because you would KNOW what was coming up for you!

Unfortunately, the reality is that you are not offered a crystal ball when you embark on this journey called life. No one knows what is going to happen in their life... ever. You can make choices and hope for the best, but your life is truly based upon your thoughts.

Do you believe there is a predestined "outline" for your life? Maybe, but instead of calling it a "predestined outline," you could call it your "karmic path." Consider this for a moment: Before your birth, you signed a contractual passport, agreeing to learn certain lessons while you were a human walking this planet.

Basically, from the time you were born until the time you die, according to this contractual passport, you have agreed that the Universe's job is to call upon you, through life experience, to fulfill your karmic path. How you choose to answer those callings is up to you. How many times you choose to experience something, to what depth, and in how many situations is also entirely up to you.

So if your future is up to you, and there isn't a predestined outline, why do you get stressed when life isn't going the way you thought it would? Remember, you thought it into being! How could you possibly be upset when life doesn't meet your expectation?

Another important note to consider is this: Your decisions are based upon your beliefs about the world and your capacity to move around in it freely. Those beliefs come from environmental programming introduced to you from the time of your birth up until now.

Truth be told, you don't need a crystal ball to clearly see where your life is headed. Instead you can benefit from calm breath, affirmative prayer, deep intuitive insight, some quiet time to recognize your path, and faith that everything is going to be OK.

Breathe and move into it. You do know where you are going because you thought it into being.

Destiny

Do you believe in destiny? What do you think it is? Do you think it is a predetermined path outlined for you before your birth? Do you think it's dependent upon outside circumstances or a plan finally working out for you? Do you think it's a predetermined future fixed on the natural order of the cosmos?

Would you be open to other ideas about destiny?

Could it be about your willingness to say yes to what you love and believe in? Could it be about your alignment with your gifts and talents and your ability to share those with the world unconditionally? Could it be about you trusting those intuitive hints and your internal guidance system when you are unsure of your next direction?

It could be all these things. One thing is for sure… it is what you make it out to be. I believe that everyone has a karmic path they signed up for with this incarnation. As human beings, we all have lessons to learn and to share. We all came here with a purpose and intention. Our destiny is what we make it out to be.

Why? Because we do have the power of choice.

Everyone gets bogged down with responsibility and obligation. In fact, responsibility and obligation distract you from your destiny! You may even have a misconception that your responsibilities and obligations ARE your destiny! But they are not. They are showing up to teach you responsibility, but most often, it's not about your destiny.

I found some really great quotes that outlined destiny a little differently:

"It's choice, not chance, that determines your destiny." —Jean Nidetch

"I can't control my destiny. I trust my soul. My only goal is just to be. There's only now, there's only here. Give in to love or live in fear. No other path, no other way. No day but today." —Jonathan Larson

"What you love and God's will for you are one and the same!" —Janet Attwood

"The purpose of life is the expansion of happiness. When it appears otherwise, you are off the path of destiny." — Janet Attwood

Your destiny is up to you… all the time. You get to choose. You get to say yes or no. You get to align yourself with the power of God and express all that is real for you in this lifetime. You get to choose between living and being.

You Are More

Whatever you are going through right now is a product of your past perceptions and beliefs about yourself and how you navigate in this world. You do understand that, right? And the only reason it is showing up as anxiety, stress, unhappiness, and inner turmoil is because you no longer subscribe to or believe in those same perceptions anymore.

So just understanding that should allow you to exhale completely and slowly. Because as you know… everything is impermanent, nothing stays the same, and this too shall pass. It may not pass without whirling things around a bit, but it will pass.

So step one: Examine what perceptions you held about yourself that brought you here and recognize that they no longer vibrate with you.

Step two: Name and adapt new ideas and affirmations about yourself and the world around you that better support where you are headed after the storm. Do you need ideas? Courage, strength, inner peace, self-love… whatever the word is for you; name it, say it, embody it.

Step three: Know that during this entire journey and perceived storm of trouble and strife, that you are more than what you are experiencing right now. The ONLY reason you are experiencing this is because your soul has called out, loud enough for you to hear, "ENOUGH IS ENOUGH! I CAN'T TAKE IT! YOU HAVE GOT TO WAKE UP TO YOUR DIVINE BEAUTY AND POWER NOW!"

I believe there is a global sense of urgency for individuals to be called to their highest good right now on the planet.

Our Earth is being raped of its preciousness. The troubles we are experiencing are self-inflicted by the ignorance of our ancestors and we are being called to get out there and do something about it before it's too late.

Help needs to be authentically connected to the Universe itself and that can only come from those individuals who are ready to drop the littleness of their lives and rise to the occasion of complete and whole aliveness and contribution to the sustainability of our world.

When you begin dropping the littleness, it creates a ripple effect to those immediately around you and it creates a little turmoil. Look beyond that turmoil. Know that the Earth is calling out to you for your help and you must understand that you are more...that is why you are being called. You are more.

Ask, Then Notice the Signs

Do you ever feel like you are wandering around aimlessly in this lifetime? Or worse yet, you are operating from such a reactionary place that you have absolutely no say in what comes next in your life?

Been there...not fun...not even a choice anymore. But that is just me—you can do what works for you.

Want to know how to shift that perception? Want to know how to actually start driving your life? Well, the first step is to understand that you are always being guided by your angels, your intuition, God, Divinity...call it what you want. There IS something larger than you and you must yield to it.

The second step would be to start asking for guidance. And honestly, you don't have to be specific in the beginning. Maybe you just simply say, "I am confused about my purpose, my path, and a decision I need to make. I could use some guidance! Please give me some guidance. I am open!"

It's not too hard to do that, right? A word of caution here: Once you affirm that you want guidance from the Universe, you are going to be inundated with answers. I mean it. It will be hard not to drop to your knees and say in surrender...ALL RIGHT! I GOT IT! THANKS! I CAN TAKE IT FROM HERE!

It will happen…almost unrelenting, actually. What could the signs look like? A billboard with an answer to a question you have been secretly asking yourself. (When I was contemplating closing my first yoga studio, I noticed a billboard that said, "'Don't be afraid. - God'." Seriously—I am not making this up.)

Random meetings with old friends or new people. Ask yourself, "Why now? Why this person?"

A loss of a friend, of money, of something you are attached to. Ask what that loss represents to you on a deeper level.

A car pulling out in front of you with a personalized license plate answering your secret question. (I had a Lexus pull out in front of me when I was asking if I should leave my marriage. The plate said, "MOVON." No lie.)

An ad popping up on your computer, a phone call coming through when you turned your phone off, weird occurrences, or chance meetings that cannot be explained.

The challenging aspect to this way of living is that you have to have faith that there are actually angels out there answering your questions or affirming your thoughts. So for those of you who always have to know how and why and need proof…substantial proof…this is going to be a tough way for you to live.

You also have to understand that these forces or Divine Guidance are so patient. They will keep sending you signs around the same topic for as long as it takes for you to believe them, have faith in yourself, and make that shift.

Life always isn't going to hand you the how. Choices aren't always going to fit perfectly into the box you decorated for yourself. The best thing you can do is ask, believe, notice, and faithfully shift.

Intuition

The sixth chakra is about seeing into your deepest sense. You shed old thought patterns and beliefs and allow your intuitive guidance system to speak louder than the voices outside. You begin to notice the voice that says, "Do you really want to believe that? Did you always believe that? Who says? Couldn't it be another way? Is this in alignment with your beliefs or someone else's? How does this belief make you feel?"

It is here where you begin seeing—internally and externally. Headaches can be a trigger for sixth chakra issues. After reviewing medical reasons for your recurring headaches, you can ask yourself the following: Do the headaches happen at certain times? Is there something going on in my life that I don't want to see? Are there buried memories from the past that are trying to surface?

The pineal gland is the spot where the third eye resides. It produces serotonin—one of the primary neurotransmitters—as well as melatonin, which influences sleep and dreams. This gland can be adversely affected by artificial lighting, stress, temperature fluctuations, magnetic fields, and radiation. You can see now why it can be challenging to not follow your intuition—it can be easily blinded by your daily activities.

From this chakra, you envision your future, but you also store your past memories. Like watching your life on a movie screen, you have memories stored in your consciousness. Some memories are pleasant while others are not. You may be holding onto traumatic events that affected your emotional well-being, and in an effort to keep those thoughts buried, you block your sixth chakra. Keep in mind that any memory you may have that is perceived as negative is most likely worse than the event itself.

For many, this chakra remains closed because most people do not take the time to focus on it. It's a lot of work to write down dreams in the middle of the night. It takes effort to visualize and meditate and it takes courage to go back in time to eradicate past memories that don't suit you anymore. You have access to intuitive insight—it starts when you are young. However, at some point in time you may have held a belief about something and a grown-up told you that your perception was wrong. If this was done continually, your intuition was not given the proper ground to blossom.

Practicing visualizations, training the mind to focus, working with dreams, and practicing detachment are the best ways to develop and balance this chakra center.

Want an exercise that can help you begin to wake up your intuition? Begin to journal your future. Visualize it as you would dream it to be. Notice the details—where you are, who you are with, even what the temperature is like and what you are wearing. Write down your visualization. Keep writing until you are thoughtless. Every day, write down something that you have visualized from your future. Begin to notice the feelings it evokes in you. Write those down, too.

One outcome of a healthy sixth chakra is the emergence of personal vision for the world and the part you play in it. It may come to you as a flash, it may happen when something pivotal manifests in your life, or it may develop over time. It often happens when you really begin to notice the issues that plague your world on a larger scale and you look for ways to rise above your own needs and serve.

Want one more exercise that can help heal and open your third eye to seeing and discerning truth from illusion? Close your eyes and see your life exactly as it is right now. Now imagine some kind of breakthrough that may happen for you. It could be anything that would radically change your life as you see it now. You don't have to know what that life looks like—you just know it has changed drastically.

Feel the physical effect that possibility has on your body. Feel the sensations in your throat, heart, and belly. Feel them grounding into the very makeup of your body. See if you can call this to mind every day during meditation and visualization—it will come to manifest.

Spiraling Out

When you do finally begin living your new definition of reality, things begin moving very fast. You have said to the Universe, "OK, I am ready! BRING IT ON!" Poof! Your life starts changing before your eyes.

It's almost as if, at the moment you said yes, a huge gust of wind began to propel you forward, and it did. It is the breath of inspiration, the breath of unity, the breath of Divine Guidance. It's blowing you in the direction of what you have chosen.

While this is going on, the people in your life and the circumstances showing up for you still remain hazy, mainly because this is all new to you, and yes, sometimes self-doubt rears its ugly head. And yes, sometimes you look behind you just to see how far you have come and of course, when you do that, you trip.

It's all good, so not to worry. It's like learning to walk all over again. You're going to fall. Just get back up again and keep moving forward.

On some days it feels like you are in the middle of this whirlwind; you are standing at the eye of the storm of your life looking into the debris being moved uncontrollably around you. You watch as people, events, and perceived problems begin spiraling out of your life.

Picture a hurricane. There is the eye of the storm in the middle...that's you. You are just standing there, calm, cool, collected, and bearing witness to all sides of your life spinning uncontrollably around you. You continue to stand in your truth as life whirls around you. You don't close your eyes, you don't recoil in fear, you don't get into the whirlwind...you just witness. You watch with love, patience, and compassion as people, events, and perceived problems spiral out.

There are a couple of things to remember here. One is that you don't have to "do" anything. Once you make the decision to move into your truth and things start spinning...stay calm and rooted. Know that the storm will pass. Secondly, make sure you are blessing those things that are spiraling out of your life. If you don't, they will show up again during the next storm of your life, only they will just look a little different. And lastly, there will be another storm. But how you handle this one will directly correlate to how strong you perceive the next one to be.

Hang on... it's only a storm.

Affirmations & Postures

The Universe only has three answers to your prayers:

Yes - Not now - I have something better in mind.

You just know that your life has to be better than the movie you are watching right now. You will know for sure it's time to make a change when you slowly exhale, knowing that everything will be OK in time.

You are going to have to fall off that tightrope and trust that the Universal net is going to catch you. You can do this without even looking down.

Pay attention to what is showing up for you. Recognize that it is a mirror of your soul. Pay attention and then make choices that are elevating and expanding.

If you ever imagine something better for yourself, you are imagining it because your heart knows it is so.

Let go of fear as you jump off the diving board into the water below, nose plugged and eyes squeezed tight. Let it happen. Know that you are safe, that you will emerge - maybe after hitting the bottom - and exhale completely.

Dancers

Eagle

Downdog

Plough

Tree

Shoulderstand

Chapter 7
On Attachment versus Co-creation
Crown Chakra: Sahasrara

Earth Shift

Does anyone else sense a stir in the Universe right now? Can you feel the change happening beneath your feet? There is profound movement in our world and I'm not talking about earthquakes… although they're quite an interesting manifestation of what is really rumbling below.

Scientifically speaking, the earth (and other planetary objects for that matter) are shifting. But if you subscribe to the belief that thoughts become things, then wouldn't it make sense that the physical shifts are taking place because of a general global unrest?

At least try to wrap your brain around this idea; maybe we didn't CAUSE the earthquake in Haiti, floods in Australia, or tsunami in Japan, BUT our thoughts are so geared toward turmoil, turbulence, conflict, and a NEED for change that collectively, could it be a manifestation of our own global thoughts and inner need for change, shifts and transformation?

Too much responsibility and not enough proof for you to fully get on board with that idea?

That's okay. You don't have to believe that little old you can actually create natural disasters on a global level. However, you can create natural disasters in your little old life. Now, the natural disasters may be a healthy shift in disguise, but the bottom line is that YOU created them. And remember, if we are all one, and everything you think and do has a ripple effect on the world around you, then I guess it just depends on how large your view of the world truly is.

Interesting to think about, isn't it? How much of an effect YOU have on the world depends on YOUR view of the world.

You're going to have to admit it… your reach IS global. It may start off small… just affecting your own little life, but then, it ripples to your community. You touch someone in your community who then spawns a shift that reaches out nationally. Then, that national outreach makes international change. International change affects the globe. And it all starts with one thought, one idea, one movement, one jostle of energy. You DO have the power. What are you going to do with it?

Surrendering to What Is

I have a very dear friend who has been diagnosed with stage four ovarian cancer. I choose my words carefully here; I deliberately did not use "struggling" or "battling" with cancer because she is doing neither of these things.

When something like illness or strife shows up in our lives, isn't our choice of words interesting? We gravitate toward words like fighting, struggling, or battling… but why? Why would we choose words that create stress and negativity? Why do we battle what shows up in our lives anyway?

Because it's not what you planned? Because it's not what you thought? Because it's uncomfortable to face? Yes… all of those things. That is the human condition—to battle what is instead of surrendering. It is the human condition to argue with what is; you know better what was meant for you, right? I mean, you make all these plans, you set goals, you strive to achieve them, and nowhere in there is illness, loss, financial hardship, or grief of any kind whatsoever. Your plan is to sail through life with no troubles or challenges. Or maybe you are okay with challenges, but not the big ones like cancer, divorce or unexpected or an unplanned death.

I went to visit this friend of mine over the weekend and I was pleasantly surprised at what I encountered. I showed up at her house and she pointed out the daffodils coming up. She told me about the huge evergreen tree that was in her yard—it was her son's first Christmas tree 24 years prior. She ate brownies and shared tea with me, and told me that she was craving macaroni

and cheese. Her purple hat fit perfectly over her gorgeously bald head. Her home was comfortable and inviting and I felt nothing less than abundance and gratitude for life.

She told me a little about how she was diagnosed, but mostly we talked about the beauty of life and how when life shifts, the best thing we can do is embrace the change and really begin to notice the gifts around us. Her outlook on life is something for everyone to adopt. And maybe, just maybe, you won't need to experience a situation of this magnitude in order to shift. Maybe you can just start today by shifting your thoughts. It takes a conscious effort to flow with the current of life and surrender to what is.

Life is about challenges…that is the human experience. And you don't get to choose how deep or difficult those challenges are. You are only meant to live through them with grace, gratitude, and reverence. Instead of taking life "by the balls," maybe you could take life in your hands and breathe it in slowly. Surrender to what is… every single bit of it.

Co-Creation

As adamantly as I subscribe to the belief that you can create your life with your thoughts, I also understand that thoughts are co-created. We create from a place of consciousness that is introduced to us through spiritual awareness and Divine Guidance.

I want to be sure I am clear with this Om so you completely understand the concept behind creating your life with your thoughts.

Creation is a joint effort to be honest. Think of it this way: your thoughts come from somewhere, right? Most of your thoughts are automatic—meaning they are repeats from earlier, the day before, the month before, the year before. They are recycled thoughts for sure.

But the new thoughts, which are few and far between, are mostly accessible through stillness and quiet. They are not about the WHAT, the HOW, or the TO BE ACCOMPLISHED. They are inspired thoughts that come from internal guidance.

BUT they can also be considered as thoughts that are coming to you from a Divine Source that KNOWS your path, KNOWS where you are going or, dare I suggest… they come from a REMEMBERED RADIANCE that can ONLY come from something bigger than yourself.

Does that make sense?

It does if you make time for stillness. It does if you can stop moving for just five minutes a day and allow yourself to be carried instead of being hell-bent on creating your life the way YOU see it going. It makes sense if you are open to letting go of ALL the responsibility that you feel the need to carry and actually admit to the fact that you make a good copilot, too.

It makes sense if you are open to allowing the Universe, God, faith, or love to carry you, especially when you don't know the way. And most of the time, you don't know the way. You think you do, but you don't. You have an idea, but your ideas are limited by your own experiences, perceptions, and judgments.

Divinity is limitless… it's ever-expanding and it knows its own nature… it CREATED nature! Think of that! Don't you want that force on your creation team? I know I do!

Let go… you don't know it all.

Courage

The words "courage" and "faith" came to me during yoga this morning. It was interesting for me to note that I have never written about courage. Not one single Om talks about courage. I have discussed fear, but never courage.

I was surprised. So here I am thinking, "What the heck am I supposed to write about courage?"

I finally looked it up online. The best definition I found was: *the quality of mind or spirit that enables a person to face difficulty, danger, pain, etc., without fear.*

Now first of all, the words "mind or spirit" interchangeably isn't working for me. They are two totally different entities, so being the yogini I am, I would like to rephrase the definition: "Courage is the quality of spirit that enables a person to face difficulty, danger, pain, etc., without fear." Because in my opinion, spirit is what guides us; the mind is what gets in our way.

How many of you actually listen to your spirit and not your mind? Your mind is that voice that barks at you and tells you not to do something because of the "WHAT IF?"

Your mind allows other people's perceptions and beliefs to influence your decision. Your mind hears old tape recordings of past doubts and worries about your abilities and capabilities. The mind is ruled by the ego and the ego hates change... it likes things to stay the same; it likes conformity.

But the spirit loves to thrive and live in the moment and be guided by passion and love and joy. The spirit is moved by how it feels... period.

The spirit doesn't have any problems... it is just in the moment, loving the ride. It doesn't worry about finances, what people think, or how things will turn out.

All that doubt, worry and judgment lives in in the mind. All those things are human conditioning. To rationalize, analyze, and make decisions based on fear or security is a learned behavior.

However, to make decisions based on self-love, passion, and connection with Universal guidance is about courage. Because why? Because these virtues or guiding principles are based in faith. Courage relies on inner-guidance or an inner knowing without "proof" of what will happen. It's like jumping through the air, swinging from the trapeze without a net, knowing you will land just fine.

It's about putting yourself out there with vulnerability and transparency, not really concerned about what people will think. You can do this because you know that you are being guided, protected and "held up" by God and Divinity. And you know that this is what IS ... so no matter what, you will be just fine.

It may feel weird the first few times you act in complete courage ... it's some-

times scary believing in your Self that much. But once you get to the other side you will see it and you will know you had "help".

Acting with courage takes determination, self-love, and a complete release of attachment to whatever the outcome.

Today, I challenge you to recognize a fear you have. And then really, truly look at it. Who would you be without that fear? Where would you be with the courage to move past your fears? What will it take to propel you into courage?

Courage is within you ... you know it… you embody it … use it. You have it in you… just do it.

Sacred Contracts

I love how the Universe works. I hope you can follow me on this one. On the same day my friend loaned me *Sacred Contracts* by Caroline Myss, I went to the secondhand bookstore and found *The Little Soul and the Sun* by Neale Donald Walsh. "Coincidence"? No….

So one night, I sat down, opened *Sacred Contracts*, and started reading the first chapter. In the most simple explanation I can share, it's about how we make contracts with other souls that will help us evolve during our humanly existence on Earth. Caroline Myss is, in my opinion, one of the most amazing women on this planet and her vision of the world is definitely God guided. It can be heavy stuff …especially at night. On this particular night, I was only able to read a few pages of the book before my eyes started to close.

Right before I fell asleep, my daughter Ava came into my room and asked me to read her book, *The Little Soul and the Sun*. I was so excited because I had wanted to read it, but she hadn't chosen it yet.

I began reading the book and immediately I realized it was a kid's version of

Sacred Contracts. It's incredibly engaging with colorful photos and large, bright words. All of a sudden, I wasn't tired anymore.

The book follows a little soul who tells God he is ready to go to Earth now. He has realized that his purpose is forgiveness and wants to start being his purpose on Earth. God explains to him that in order to know forgiveness, he must understand the complete opposite. He tells him that we can't know the light (which is natural in all of us) until we know the darkness. He tells him that he will need help understanding the opposite of forgiveness.

Another little soul comes along and says, "I will help you know forgiveness. But you must remember that it is me—the one who truly loves you—when I act mean and do things to hurt you so you can forgive me."

I began to feel so many emotions while I read this book. I don't care who you are; colorful pictures help so much in conveying any message. I say, get your copy today and read it. In one little book my heart was reminded that:

- I am a gorgeous, bright light that has the ability to shine incessantly.

- I have a purpose.

- The people who trigger me are actually LEADING me to my purpose! AND they love me!

- I always have God right by my side.

How I wish this book had been read to me over and over again as a child. How beautiful, right? Would YOU look at life differently if you had been reminded of these things as a child?

Well, here's your chance… I offer these affirmations to you. I invite you to copy the list of affirmation above and post it somewhere—everywhere! This is important because this is why you are here! And if you already know all this, look me in the eye and tell me you don't need reminding. We all do—we are human.

A couple more delicious aspects to all of this was that; one, I had just asked for guidance and understanding on this very topic, and two, not only did it fall into my lap, but it fell into my lap twice, once as an adult and once as a child.

Thankfully, *The Little Soul and the Sun* spoke directly to my soul in only 20 pages.

Crack Your Shell

I was in a yoga class once, lying in Savasana, and the instructor said, "Imagine you are in a shell and if you move, you will crack your shell. So really, try not to move at all here."

Now, as a yoga instructor, I totally get this analogy. As humans, being still is an important aspect of connecting to our spirit. And for the most part, we will do anything to keep from being still.

I agree, one thousand percent, that stillness is paramount in knowing thyself. Stillness is vital in discerning between taking action or remaining complacent. Stillness is what I like to call your "refueling station." You can completely fill your "spiritual energy tank" in Savasana, meditation, or just sitting still with your emotions as they happen.

When you are offered quiet time, take advantage of that time. Sometimes, it's the only time you will get pure peace and quiet. My kids don't think of quiet time as a punishment; to them, it's a reward. I like that way of thinking, don't you?

But on this particular day I was going through my own turmoil and my mind began racing when the instructor made that statement. I thought, "But what if I WANT to crack my shell? What if it's time to crack my shell and open up to a new paradigm of living? Then can I move?"

For some of you who practice this type of living, you become acutely aware when it's time to shift. You feel weird physically and energetically. On some days, it feels like you may be watching a movie as you move throughout your day. You begin to feel the energy coursing through your body, especially in stillness, urging you to move. Your nerves feel like they are on fire, your muscles may ache, and your heart might race.

You know that you have been living in a shell that has served you up until now. You are outgrowing the space that you have been inhabiting and it's really, really dark and cramped. The only way to make space is to crack it open yourself.

It's then that you know: It's time to move, time to crack your shell. Taking that time in stillness has allowed you the opportunity to see yourself as your Self...as you are NOW. You know that you are no longer the person that you were.

You will know that it's time because you have sat with your fear, your guilt, your shame, your grief, your lies, your illusions, and your attachments, and you have healed each and every part of your energy body, as much as you need to to finally move...you are ready.

You know it's time... there is no doubt about what is on the outside of that shell because you know that it's all FOR you.

In case you aren't getting this, it means to metaphorically crack your old ways of thinking, the old version of yourself, and your place in this world. It means cracking through old beliefs and illusions of what is real for you. These old things are keeping you cramped and suffocated; they are holding you back from the light and the space that is available to you right now.

Crack your shell... your entire being is waiting... waiting for you to expand and open up to a new, lighter version of yourself. It's time...

God 's Gift

Most of you know that I am blessed with these two amazing little girls that I seriously love more than anything I have ever loved in my life. They are the reason I get up and do my best every single day.

So you may find it interesting to note that when I got pregnant with my first daughter, Isabella, I really had no idea what the hell I was doing being pregnant. I mean, what the heck did I know about raising a child? NOTHING!

And I got pregnant with her just after September 11, 2001. Nothing like a little world trauma to instill into that DNA....poor baby. I remember saying out loud, "Well God must think I have something to offer. He never gives us more than we can handle right?" (Like I was asking for confirmation, mind you.)

Before I got pregnant, I wanted to travel the world. I wanted no attachments, no commitments and no responsibilities. My mother said I lived like a vagabond and my father said I was full of wanderlust. Judgments yes, but spot on at the time.

So, I have this baby and I am freaking out...for real. I have no idea how to change her diaper, wipe her butt, feed her or what to do to get her to stop crying. It was a terrible first few months. (maybe longer but I don't want to admit that right now.) I have this picture of her and I where she has this look of terror in her eyes. Like she made such a mistake choosing me as her mom! However, I am smiling from ear to ear, trying to capture this look like, "I know what I am doing...REALLY!"

Now, before you start tossing around judgments about me and my parenting methods, before you un-friend me or unsubscribe from my Weekly Oms, hear this. My unrest ended once I found yoga. Not right away mind you, but over time, I became very comfortable with being a mother. In fact, when God dropped my second angel, Ava, into my life, I began a monumental shift and it all started with yoga.

I will NEVER claim to be the best mom in the world... but I do my best on every day that I am given the chance. Over time, I shifted the ridiculous notion that I wasn't worthy enough to be a mother. Not only was I worthy but I was also more than capable to share my gifts, talents and Divine love with these two angels.

I changed my perception about what it meant to be a mother. And my idea of a "good mom" had nothing to do with what my mother, sister or friends thought. I stopped listening to what other people were telling me to do and I started listening to my own intuition.

I stopped carrying this ridiculous idea of perfection. My kids are resilient, perfectly imperfect and they can handle the world around them...better than some of us adults can honestly.

I recognized that maybe, just maybe, God gave them to me because they had an important message for me. Maybe my children picked me. As a parent, have you ever thought about that? I know some of you have. It's a wonderful way to shift your parenting approach.

You never know how your life will turn out. But you can look at every single thing that happens to you as a blessing from the Universe, from God, from the world as part of a Divine plan to learn something wonderful about yourself.

Thank you God for the gifts of my girls. They are a true miracle.

The Baby Chick

Everyone on this planet, admittedly or not, is experiencing a heavy-duty shift. Some of you are very awake to it, some of you are pressing the snooze button, and some of you are snoring right through it. It's all good no matter where you are, so not to worry if what I am about to say is foreign to you.

The world is shifting and we are being offered major opportunities to wake up and share our gifts, talents, and love with the world. We can no longer be smothered by technical difficulties beyond our control.

We can no longer blame anyone for our lack of growth and evolution. It's time to respond appropriately to our calling and move into it with grace, acceptance, and faith.

It's a new Earth and this new Earth cannot tolerate laziness, unconsciousness, separateness, victimization, or purposeful ignorance. Am I making any sense here? The new Earth seeks Oneness, cooperation, unconditional love, inner peace, and constant joy.

You have been programmed to navigate through this life in a certain way. This programming comes from your parents, your environment, and your

upbringing… all relatable to what you adapted as patterned thoughts, behaviors and beliefs.

Most of these behavioral patterns have kept you alive and surviving. But for the most part, they are keeping you from thriving in this new Earth. A lot of what we have learned can no longer vibrate at the level of frequency that the new Earth is working on.

Maybe this will help… a baby chick grows in an egg, right? In order for that baby chick to experience the new Earth, it must peck through his tough shell in order to SEE the new Earth.

The baby chick doesn't have anyone telling him when it's time to start pecking; he just knows when it's time. There is no question about why he must start pecking, he just knows he has to; it's the next stage of his evolution. He has no idea what lies on the other side; for all he knows, there could be a huge cat waiting for him to come out so he can have his dinner.

The point is… you may not know when, why, or how you are to move into your next stage of evolution. You will know when the time is right and you will move.

For some people, it's now. For others, it's already happened. For some, the snooze button is still more appealing.

Whatever road you take, you will have to get out of that egg at some point… it's going to get cramped and very uncomfortable. You just have to decide when enough is enough and you need more space… just like the chick.

Bring on the Wonder

When you are stripped of all familiarity and perceived security, you can't help but wonder… what's next? You've gotten through the fear of letting go, past the turmoil of minute details, you've surrendered to the next stage of your evolution, and the only question that comes to mind now is… what's next?

The truth is no one knows what is next at any given point in time. However, I think it's safe to say that the ONLY way to experience wonder is to allow space for it.

And to be honest… you may not have to lose or compromise one single thing to understand this concept.

You can wake up each day with this thought. How great would that be? To wake up every single day and say… *bring on the wonder! I can't wait to see what is going to unfold for me today!*

You can do this, you know. You have the choice and the freedom to experience bliss and wonder every day of your life. Even for those of you who are in very predictable, mundane lives right now… there is wonder all around you.

Where?

In nature. In a stranger's glance. In a new way to drive to work. In your child's eyes. In a new hairstyle. In a new food. In a new radio station. In your breath.

It's there… wonder. Just look for it—it will fall right into your lap… several times a day if you let it.

The Car Ride

When you are beginning to grow in your spiritual awareness, some people who once resonated with you begin to drop away from your conscious circle. It's nothing to be sad about, mourn, or feel bad about... it's a natural progression of your own spiritual evolution.

You won't be able to talk the same language anymore. You won't like the same things anymore. Your awareness of what is real and your interests shift and if you keep in mind that nothing is permanent, it's all okay!

Additionally, remember that every single person on this planet has a path. And their path is different from yours. Your paths can't possibly be the same... you are uniquely you and they are uniquely them! It's the way the world works!

This is why you work toward eliminating judgment from your thoughts. You can't judge other people and why they make the choices they make, or why they do the things they do. It's not your business.

This is an easy process—the dropping away—when you are talking about a stranger, co-worker, distant relative, or a friend that you don't see that often. They aren't in your face every single day, so their choices don't affect you and yours need not affect them. It's simple.

However, what happens when someone close to you is staying complacent in their growth and you are spirituality alive and growing? Then what? Did you feel that flip in your stomach? That's because there is a need to take action on your part, but there is fear and turmoil about what to do.

I equate this situation to a car ride. When this happens, do you put the car in neutral, stalling your own growth, hoping they will catch up? Do you feel like

you are sticking your head out the driver's side window saying, "Hey, c'mon! This is going to be fun!" If you are doing that now, stop it. It's self-defeating to you and demeaning to the other person.

You can't hope they will "catch up" to you. Maybe their path is completely different from yours. Allow them that space to grow on their own. Maybe they want to go down the dirt road and not get on the freeway… you don't know!

Maybe you put the car in reverse and back up to get them. It's not too far back there and honestly, you love this person, so it's worth the time, right? Maybe they will learn something from this simple act of kindness and self-sacrifice you just demonstrated. ACK! No way! That is NOT spiritual growth—that is saying in clever way, "I am better than you and I am going to give you another chance to see it. Now get in!" Not OK.

The only way to deal with this type of thing when it happens is to continue along your path and go at a pace that is comfortable for you. It's YOUR journey regardless of what role they have played in your life up until now. It's THEIR journey regardless of what role you have played in their life up until now. Stalling or reversing won't work for either of you. Your journey together may be over for this lifetime… or it may cross at certain junctions along the way.

It just is what it is. All spiritual growth comes with some separation. It's okay… let go and keep driving.

The Root System

Close your eyes for a moment and imagine a gorgeous forest full of trees— all kinds of trees towering overhead. They are amazing… you look up and you can't tell where one starts and one ends. You look down and the trunks themselves are obviously separate as they burrow into the ground. Their

trunks are sturdy and stoic as they stand alone.

If you were to take a look underneath the earth, you would see their root system.

Their root system connects them to the nourishment of the Earth. They need the Earth to sustain them and grow. Not only that, but they also need the natural elements of sunshine and water… something they have no control over but use as needed to sustain their life. As a unit, working together, they have created an ecosystem that relies on them for their survival as well. It's really quite profound if you think about it in this way.

When you look deeper into the Earth you notice that the root system of this forest is interconnected. It's actually a web of roots. The trees have been here so long that their roots are intertwined and they share the same space without struggle. There is enough to go around for every single tree.

If one tree gets pulled up, let's say, by its roots… the entire system will be affected. In some way, shape, or form, every single tree will be affected. Not only that, but the ecosystem is affected as well. And the amount of rain and sun that the surrounding trees are subject to has changed, shifting the entire forest on a level none of us can see.

Keeping your thoughts with this forest, ask yourself this question… what makes you different from those trees? They are a creation of nature, right? And so are you, right? So how are you any different from those trees?

The answer is you aren't any different. You are exactly the same. And not only that, but everything you think, feel, and do affects the general area around you. Your energy and your thoughts have a ripple effect on the entire Universe. Don't believe me? That's fine. You don't have to. But ask yourself what that choice of denial sends out into the Universe. What type of energy vibration is denial? Is it a flow or a blockage? Is it a surrender or a fight against what is?

What happens when you make a choice? You affect the entire flow of the Universe. Why? Because we are all connected through an intricate web of energy roots. We are all connected. In this big, big world, little old you makes choices every day that either sustain the peace, harmony, and love of the world or don't. The wonderful thing to remember is that *you have a choice*.

We are connected. We are part of something much bigger than ourselves. Accept it, yield to it, and stop sweating the small stuff like a dropped acorn, peeled-back bark, a rabbit hole through your trunk, or the change of the

seasons. YOU ARE PART OF AN ENTIRE UNIVERSE THAT IS CON-NECTED.

What are you going to do now?

Where Are We Headed?

Since we are diving into the Crown Chakra, I would like to introduce a thought about our interconnectedness.

Take a look at the world around you and ask yourself where do YOU think we are headed? Big question, I know. Let me be more specific if I can.

Where do you think we are headed in our political arena with regard to energy security, the climate change, the coral reefs, the rainforest, unrest in Africa and the Mideast?

What about the global financial crises, world hunger and poverty, racism, and global warming? What about the systems we have in place now for our aging population here in the United States? Or the failing educational system for our children? What would happen if you took a look in your own little community? What is happening in your own backyard? Drugs, teenage suicide, pregnancy, rising health care, home foreclosures, divorce...

The world is such a nasty place, isn't it?

What can you do? Talk about daunting. Nothing, in my opinion, is more daunting than the road our world is currently traveling down. And really, if you try to take it all in with your breath, you are going to choke. I am very good at breathing and I choke ... literally.

So how about we release the grip we have on NEEDING to FIX everything and CHANGE THE WORLD.

Let's just say for a moment that we are all One. And let's just believe that even one little person can make one little change. None of us are here to CHANGE the world. However, we are ALL here to notice where *our* gifts, talents, abilities and passion line up with a *need* in our world. Everyone has the power to make small changes. And what do you think happens when everyone makes small changes within THEMSELVES?

Yes the whole world changes. WE may not see it in our lifetime but our children will, our children's children will and if you believe in reincarnation you will get to experience this world from an entirely different perspective on your next go around.

The world issues are knocking at your door to be more, contribute more and show up fully present and aware. That doesn't mean you have to tackle it all at one time. You'll die a quick death. It just means choose. Choose what you are passionate about and focus on that.

The world needs you, your spouse, your family, your friends and your community. Find your passion and inspire others around you to do the same. THAT is how we make global shifts.

How Deep is Your Sleep?

The world consciousness is waking up. It's a fact that can't be denied. If you are reading this, you are waking up—or maybe you have been awake and you're just curious about what I have to say today.

Either way, just by reading this Om, you have chosen a path of spiritual connection, divine guidance, conscious choices, and understanding your passionate purpose! Isn't that fun? Bet you didn't know what you were getting yourself into, did you?

Honestly, you can take these Oms for what they are and what they mean to you. Maybe it's a nice read in the morning with your coffee and bagel; or

something you scan over prior to going to bed at night. Maybe you open up this book to a random page on random days for guidance. However you choose to use read these Oms, I am honored and feel very blessed that you have taken the time read my thoughts! The wonderful thing though about these is that you have the choice to interpret what they mean to you and how you will or will not incorporate the information into your life.

What does it really mean to me that you are reading these? Why am I so excited about it?

It means that you are awake. It means that you are open and receptive to new ideas about yourself, the world around you, your beliefs, and how you navigate through this lifetime. It means that you understand, on some level, that you are connected to all of the power, love, and glory that is infinitely available to you and to everyone else around you! It means that on some level, you recognize that you are not separate from anything the world has to offer you.

It means that you believe, on some level, that life is abundant and that you have unlimited access to all the gifts that you can dream up for yourself.

However…there are various levels of sleeping. You can decide for yourself where you are on this spectrum.

The first level of sleeping is a deep and intoxicated sleep, when you are sleeping so deeply that you believe in separation and isolation; you are bumping into everyone while you try to find the person to blame for your misfortune.

The second level of sleeping is a nice, long nap. This is where you go in and out of consciousness. You enjoy the fact that you are connected and alive, but on some days, it just becomes a bit too much for you. In order to counteract that feeling of overall responsibility for your thoughts and actions, you take naps.

Your nap could look like watching too much mindless television, distracting yourself with impure thoughts, eating unnecessarily and past the point of being full, yelling at your kids, or blaming others for your problems.

Then there is a high-light sleep where you are really sleeping with one eye open at all times. You know that you are connected; you feel it, live it, and express it. You rejoice in the fact that you understand all of this, but sometimes you do trip yourself up. But it's only because you got in your own way!

You fully understand that you have the power to love fully, be showered with abundance, and have unlimited access to Universal Powers.

Some call this allowing God to live through you as you. I call it super-fun living, and it's available to every single person on this planet. But you have to wake yourself up. You have to decide, without judgment, which one works best for you.

I can say this honestly—as a spiritual being navigating through this life as a human being, you may vacillate between all three at any given time.

However, now that you are even a little bit awake, you never have the choice to go fully back to sleep again! Your snooze button is officially broken… How's that for you?

Eternal Discovery

I am so in love with these two words together. Don't they just make your heart sing and your exhale come out slowly and completely? They do for me. Eternal discovery… ahh…

I think this may be why I fell in love with the practice of yoga. It's a never-ending well of knowledge, insight, self-discovery, and applicable tools for living consciously.

And for those of you not even remotely interested in the philosophy of yoga, the poses are fun to learn and practice! Especially the ones that provide the most challenge for you! Because when you finally get upside down in Sirsasana (Headstand) or hold Bakasana (Crow Pose) for more than a nanosecond, you feel a rush of energy and accomplishment!

So, as always, I would like to relate our eternal discovery on our mats to our eternal discovery off our mats.

Say you are brand new to yoga. Never done it before, totally afraid, anxious to try it, and nervous about everything about yoga. You can't touch your toes, you have no idea what Surya Namaskar (Sun Salutation) is, so you really don't

want to do it eight times. But here you are... in the front row of a new yoga class.

Now what? You begin a brand new discovery about yourself as a physical being. After a few classes (or weeks or months) you notice that your hamstrings are a little looser, your quads are a little stronger, that ache in your shoulders is gone, and you haven't had one single headache in over a month! It's amazing!

You are stronger than you have ever been! In fact, you can't believe it, but you actually tried Astavakrasana (8 Angle Pose). You fell on your face, but you tried it! And you can't wait to try it again!

What have you learned here, if this is you? That you can touch your toes and no one cares what you look like or if you fall.

The physical benefits of yoga are truly unlimited. You pushed yourself to your edge in your pose and maybe even beyond what you thought you could do. Basically moving past limiting beliefs you had about your physical ability when you started this practice. That is empowering, isn't it?

So now you are a dedicated yogi (or yogini) and you love it so much, you are going to class three times a week. You have given up coffee because it makes your heart beat too fast in yoga. You haven't had any fast food since you started this practice either, because it makes you feel like you might fart in class. And when you know you are going to class in the morning, you refrain from drinking any alcohol because you know class will be that much more challenging.

What have you learned here, if this is you? That you are beginning to make conscious choices about what you consume based on feeling good. Interesting—that's all— just interesting.

So off you go... it's been about six months now and you are so totally into your yoga practice. You love it! It's really making you feel great on the outside. So you get into Ustrasana (Camel Pose) and all of a sudden your heart feels like it's going to explode and you can't believe it but you have tears rolling down your cheeks! Holy shit! What the hell is going on? You come out of the pose and rest in Balasana (Child's Pose) to get ahold of yourself. You get through the rest of the class without crying until you finally rest in Savasana (Corpse Pose). The tears just won't stop.

What have you learned here, if this is you? You've learned that you are layers of density and you just accessed your deepest layers of being—your energy

system—through the practice of yoga. You just began, without knowing it, an eternal discovery of your innermost spiritual being, through the practice of yoga.

This journey will never end because you are an ever-evolving being that changes and shifts with the flow of life. But just know, this is only the beginning... you took the first step of discovery to a new you.

Ahhhhhhhhhhhhhhhhhhhhhhhhhhhhhhhhh...

Breathing

Are you skeptical about the thought that we are all One? Can I offer you a mediation that may help you with this one?

OK... here we go. Sit in an easy, comfortable position. Make sure you don't have to use much muscular energy to accomplish this. So lean against a wall if you have to; prop your hips up with a blanket if you have to— whatever it takes to be super comfortable.

Now close your eyes and begin to breathe. Breathe in through the nose and out through the nose. Notice the coolness of the breath as you take it in. Focus on the lungs and how full you can make them on your inhale and then truly, how empty you can make them on your exhale.

Maybe begin counting to a slow count of six when you breathe in and out. Think of the breath as an infinite and constant movement of energy that you direct but that you really have no control over.

Do this for about five minutes. The mind will want to play with you a little bit here, but just blow the thoughts away and save them for later. They are not important right now.

After about five minutes of breathing begin to imagine your spouse, partner, best friend, children, and family members all sitting with you, breathing along with you in this same space. You are all just sitting there, breathing in unison.

It's beautiful because the sound of your breath combined makes beautiful music. It sounds like the ocean, actually—as smooth and natural as the waves when they come in and go out along the shore.

Do this for about five minutes, thinking about nothing but you and the most important people in your life breathing right alongside you.

Then after those five minutes, you will begin to imagine their friends, their school mates, and the families of their friends and schoolmates all breathing alongside you. Now your collective breathing really takes on a life of its own.

In fact, the power of your breath combined actually begins to move in unison with the gentle breeze in the trees. And it moves in unison with the natural gravitational pull of the waves as they lap onto the shore. There is no separation between you, your family, your friends, their friends, and your connection with nature.

It's all a constant movement of energy and natural breath. That's what I'm talking about... that feeling.

Ahhhhhhhhhhhhhhhhhh... feel it, surrender to it... we are all One.

Emerging As Your Self

Anyone else feel like every day offers you a chance to change the way you view yourself? Anyone else ever look in the mirror and notice subtle differences about your physical self? Anyone else admit to a shift in what you allow to bother you now on any given day? Anyone else FEEL like a new person when you wake up?

You are a new person each time you wake up! You are changing physically, emotionally, and spiritually every single day! Well, you have the opportunity to shift every day, whether you take that opportunity or not is entirely up to you.

The world is moving at a speed that offers you countless opportunities to shift and move toward your most authentic Self. It's you who has to make the choice to accept or deny these opportunities.

Do you want to continue to live in the same patterns, behaviors, and stories that keep you right where you are? Or are you ready for a more authentic, joyful way of living?

That's the question you really have to ask yourself. Have you recognized the stories you live by and do they resonate with you now? Or are they old and stagnant? If they are, it's time to break free of them and move on to something different.

But even if your life is seemingly "perfect" and you are free from old stories and negative self-talk, you still are offered opportunities to shift. You are still offered situations to shine brighter.

The question then becomes this: How bright DO you want to shine? Can you stand the light being so bright?

You can if you know that you are perfect where you are… no matter what. You can if you know how to share. You can if you know how to live in reverence and gratitude.

You can if you can be open to the consequences of being vulnerable and transparent. And it's not always pretty either. People will question you, belittle you, challenge you and maybe even put you down for emerging as this "new you."

How strong are you? Can you stand on your own two feet in confidence and graceful strength…offering up nothing more than who you are right now? With no expectations, no belief that you are better or worse, just that you are YOU..right now. Can you stand there and be okay with people not liking you anymore, questioning you and maybe trying to "take you down"?

If you aren't … just take a quick look in the mirror. Look deep into your eyes and believe you are that strong. Believe you are that powerful! Believe you are that connected and believe that it is time!

Allow your Self to emerge. It's waited a long time and it's time to shine people. The world needs brightness… it's been living in darkness for too long.

Stop waiting… it's serving no one.

Instant Manifestation

I've said it before and some of you already see it happening. The world is spinning at a very rapid rate. Your thoughts are becoming things almost instantly. Have any of you recognized that yet? Nothing, and I mean nothing, is a coincidence. It's all your thoughts… manifesting instantly into what you believe to be true.

If you ever hear yourself say, "What a coincidence!" take a breath and think about what you thought, said, or did to create that "coincidence." I presume this could very well be a HUGE aha moment for most of you.

If you can recognize and believe that you have the power to create, this knowledge can produce such a huge shift in your life.

So let me ask you, what do you think about all day? Are your thoughts centered on gratitude and reverence? Do they show up as love for all that is? Are your thoughts open to how you can be more, do more, and show up more in alignment with who you really are at a soul level?

Or instead, do you wonder how you got into the circumstance you are currently in? Or are you trying to figure out how to change the people or circumstances around you so that you can finally feel joy?

Or maybe, you want to just get OVER your situation and just survive another day already! Maybe if you stop thinking about it, it will just go away. Any of you resonate with this?

Change your thoughts. YOU are the one creating your own reality. YOU are the one who is using your thoughts, which follow with words, which follow with actions, to create your life. Only YOU can change it. And it doesn't mean you have to compromise, become a doormat, or look the other way. What it does mean is that you have to discipline your thoughts, which means you have to recognize them first. That is a huge task when you have over 70,000 thoughts a day. You can't possibly discipline or discern all of them… or can you?

Maybe not all of them, but the breath sure can help. Take time every single day to notice what you are thinking about. Stop before you speak. Listen to your words when you do speak. Evaluate your actions. It's called conscious living… moving with intention, purpose, and passion. Anyone can walk around this earth as a human being, but YOU have the opportunity to INSTANTLY create your life… with just your thoughts.

I don't know why I am seriously awestruck when I test this theory over and over again. I get the same results every single time but it still amazes me on such a deep level.

When you sit, even for a minute, every single day and allow thoughts to come to you, you are opening the flood gates of creation. You are saying on a very ethereal level, "I am ready". When you then take that time and consciously direct your thoughts on an intention … it will manifest… almost immediately. It's not tricky…try it if you haven't already.

Make certain your thoughts are exactly what you are envisioning. Or better yet, ask the questions that will help you grow and see what comes next. I can guarantee you, what happens within minutes to an hour to a day/two, will show up exactly as you thought it to be.

Powerful Shifts

I get so excited around the holidays and the approaching New Year! Yes, the holidays are super fun with two little girls who still believe in Santa Claus.

Their faces light up when I drag out the decorations. They can't wait to go through the bins and scatter them all over the family room. Our heirloom Cookie Cookbook has small sticky notes on almost every page so I know which cookies they want to make. And every morning my girls put all the inside Christmas lights on before they even eat breakfast. I love it—especially when it's cold and dark outside.

I still get excited at Christmas but mainly the holiday excitement is about them. Personally, I get caught up in the energy of the upcoming New Year beyond the holiday hoopla. I love the anticipation of what is yet to come. I have always been one of those people who thrive on change. I actually get excited when I can say, "Gosh, where will my life be six months from now?"

The New Year offers you a marked time and date when you can let go of the old and make space for the new. I used to write goals each New Year. Before kids, my aspirations included trips to exotic places, career objectives, and usually financial ideals. I still make a New Year list, but it looks very different now.

Overall though, the New Year represents the one guarantee in life we all share—impermanence. And to be perfectly honest, each moment, regardless of the date, offers that powerful insight, if you are open to it.

You can shift your life on any given day, in every given moment. And you can fall into each moment as it is, knowing that it will pass… whether or not you were present in it. Every moment in your life is different from the last.

Your life as you see it right now will change. It's inevitable; it has to change! However, the New Year is a chance to make declarations about how your life will shift when the clock strikes midnight.

But the truth is that in every moment of every day, you are making declarations to the Universe and shifting your life—New Year or not. Every single moment offers you an opportunity to change direction.

So continue to use the stroke of midnight on December 31 as a marker for change. But please, understand that you have that same power in every moment of your life. Wake up to this this coming year… create powerful shifts all year long!

Don't Wait to Share Your Gifts

Some of you mistakenly think that because you do not have it all "together," that you have nothing to share. This couldn't be further from the truth. Think about this for a moment.

We are human beings, right? We are constantly evolving and growing into new versions of our Selves, right? Our evolution is a lifelong journey, right? So if you wait until you have it all "together," you may be too tired or ill to speak your truth about what you know.

Does this make sense?

In every moment of your life, you know exactly what you need to know. Not only that, but in every moment you are perfect. AND you have everything you need to share amazing insight, information, and love with everyone you meet. At any given moment, someone in your immediate circle of consciousness NEEDS to hear something you have to say or experience something you have to offer.

It's true! Too often we keep our mouths shut for fear of looking like we don't know it all. We CAN'T know it all! Even when we die, we won't know it all! So why wait to share what you know NOW!

As you trek along this personal journey called your life, keep in mind that God created you perfectly. From the day you were born until now, you have embodied perfection, love, and harmony with the Universe around you.

The people and circumstances you experience are a direct reflection of where you are right now in your life. AND they are brought to you by your own thinking because they are something your soul wishes to experience and learn from.

There are no accidents, coincidences, or happenstance— everything is in Divine Order—all the time.

So if you hold out and refuse to share YOUR gifts of love, knowledge, wisdom, insight, faith, and joy with the immediate world around you, what do you think happens? Well, you take away from the true experience of this lifetime for yourself and also for those around you.

Don't be afraid to share your gifts… the world is waiting. And your gifts will change throughout your lifetime. The way you think, speak, and love will all shift, but only if you share what you know right now.

Get out there already! The world is waiting!

A New Paradigm

The hip expression "a new paradigm" is floating around. Have you heard it? What exactly does it mean?

I've heard people use the phrase, "Our world is shifting into a new paradigm" or "Are you ready to become a new version of your Self in this new paradigm?"

What do they mean, anyway?

I'm a little confused only because I thought that the world only shifted according to our perceptions—that it really wasn't shifting; it was just our thoughts that were shifting.

So if that is the case, then how come we can say that our world is shifting into a new paradigm? If it's only our thoughts that shift, can we admit that the world really isn't shifting—just our awareness to certain aspects is shifting?

Maybe the standards we have agreed to in the past about what works with regard to money, relationships, career choices, environmental sustainability, and even love or family are all different now.

Maybe what we used to believe or the concepts we used to subscribe to aren't really beneficial in the world as it is now. Could that be the case?

You know what I think? I think that the world IS shifting into a new paradigm. And it has everything to do with your thoughts, but on a much larger level then you or I could conceive.

You know why? Because enough people are tired of living a lie. Enough people are tired of trying to keep up with a lifestyle that is not what they want. Enough people are sick of doing what they were told to do and are instead listening to their hearts. Enough people are being authentic about who they are, which in turn is attracting more authentic people, which in turn is creating a sort of global boycott to sameness, complacency, separation, and anxiety about the future.

There IS a new paradigm and it starts with YOUR thoughts. Believe that your thoughts create change; your thoughts create new paradigms; your thoughts affect other people, who in turn affect other people.

Move into the new paradigm. Don't worry whether or not it's the "hip" one or the one for you. Just navigate with your heart instead of your mind and everything wonderful will follow.

The Branch

When you begin growing into the "new paradigm" of your Self and things start shifting, the bottom beneath you feels like it is falling. And it feels that way because it is.

Everything that you once knew and believed to be true is falling away and you no longer feel supported. You feel like you are just hanging out there, on limb, by a thread, whatever you want to call it… and it feels that way because you are.

What is your gut instinct? Fear. You feel very fearful... this is all unfamiliar territory. Your first reaction may be to cling to the old ways of thinking and being. Your reaction is to go "back" and find what is comfortable and safe.

My question is this: How many times have you done that before? And how did that work for you? Can you look back on your life and witness the times when you have retreated in fear, only to find yourself in the very same position you are in right now?

You're in the same position because it's history repeating itself. It's the Universe giving you the same instance over and over again until you finally get the lesson. It's a game your ego plays to keep you "safe."

But you aren't safe in complacency and sameness. You aren't safe in your old ways of thinking and being. It seems safe because it's familiar, but familiar doesn't always bring about joy, fulfillment, bliss, and connection. Faith does. But falling into faith requires experiencing fear first.

Think of it this way: When you feel like you are out on the limb between your new and your old life, you are traversing between the unconscious ways that you have been living and the new conscious ways you are experiencing in glimpses now. The thing is, once you have experienced consciousness, once you have awoken from your deep slumber of sedated living, you cannot go back.

The new beliefs that come from your heart are speaking loudly now and the ego is trying hard to invalidate them and keep you in sameness. To be honest, the battle gets a little ferocious at times. You retreat and then you charge forward and retreat again and charge forward again.

And this goes on and on until you finally say, "Enough is enough is enough. I trust... I have faith... I know that the ground beneath me has shifted. I know that I am hanging out here on a limb. But I know that once I let go, I will see the clear path to my new life and the new me. And it IS in alignment with who I am becoming. It's OK to let go."

You just have to let go of that branch and trust that the Universe will catch you. It's all going to be OK.

You Just Have to Trust

When you really and truly say "Yes!" to God, to the Universe, and to living your life empowered and alive, you have signed a verbal contract to shift.

Now, as far as I know, there is no such thing as a written contract with God and to this day, I have never read any "fine print" about what will happen once you say yes. You can't really know what is coming up next for you when you agree to hold hands with a Higher Power… you just have to trust.

Sometimes the shift is fairly simple and sometimes the people who are closest to you in your life want to shift along with you. But from what I have witnessed personally, usually when you shift and say yes, you are required to drop a few belongings. It's like leaving your luggage with a porter, but when you leave it, you have to leave it for good. It may be there later for you to pick up; the question is… do you want it back or not?

It may be that you lose a business, change jobs, leave a marriage, move from your home, or change your environment completely. You can't know any outcome and you can't plan when you say yes to God… you just have to trust.

This is challenging for people who have been living an illusion of control their entire life. But if you can remember that control IS an illusion and that Divine Guidance is carrying you all the time, it's OK. It's OK to let go… it's actually freeing because you begin to FEEL weightless and open.

You witness your thoughts and you experience life ushering you along, but you also know that you are being guided by the hand of God.

You know that God lives in your heart and that your heart cannot experience pain, grief, anger, resentment, guilt, or anything that makes you feel less than blissful and connected, so you know it's OK to let God express bliss and Oneness through you.

But you can't control it. You can't drive. You can't say where to turn, which road to take, or what you have to leave behind… you just have to trust.

I know it's hard… I did it. I closed a business, lost money, foreclosed on a house, and left a marriage, all in a matter of two years. With all that baggage, I relinquished a dimension of myself that was hurt, angry, guilty, shameful, and fearful of allowing. I abandoned a dimension of myself who wanted love but didn't trust love. I gave up a dimension of myself who wanted to trust but wasn't sure how.

It's not easy. But you have to know, way deep down in your heart of hearts, in your God heart, that you are going to be OK. You have to know that when you leave everything behind, you open yourself up to pure love, pure joy, pure happiness, endless patience, reverence for life, eternal gratitude, and a blissful existence. You open yourself up to all that you could hope for and more.

You will still encounter human experiences; however, this time you are closely connected with your own Spirit, with God, with the flow of the Universe, and with the angels, so you know that no matter what happens you are supported.

Never again will you feel the need to control anything… you will always be able to let it flow.

Let's do this already, shall we?

Affirmations & Postures

Let go, surrender, let nature take its course with your life. Be firm in your ground but open to the beauty within.

Elevate your own consciousness so you can react from a place that is aligned with your soul. This raises the collective consciousness and allows others to do the same.

Listen in times of uncertainty; create stillness and begin navigating your life from your soul.

Embrace darkness…it always leads to the light.

Instead of taking life "by the balls," maybe you could take life in your hands and breathe it in slowly.

Divinity is limitless… it's ever-expanding and it knows its own nature… it CREATED nature! Think of that! Don't you want that force on your creation team?

Crack your shell… your entire being is waiting… waiting for you to expand and open up to a new, lighter version of yourself.

Whatever road you take, you will have to get out of that egg at some point… it's going to get cramped and very uncomfortable. You just have to decide when enough is enough and you need more space… just like the chick.

Bridge

Camel

Fish

Plank

Plough

Wheel

About The Author

Dana Damara has embraced yoga as a lifestyle both on and off the mat. Through her children, writing, and creation of meaningful relationships with the community around her, Dana has facilitated that power of soulfulness and spiritual awakening through yoga, both for others and herself.

Damara moves and breathes with the breath of the Universe. She thrives in the face of adversity, understanding that everything that happens *to* us, actually happens *for* us. She dances with meditation and yoga, knowing that this practice alone helps to protect the mind from distractions that keep us from our most vibrant path.

She is guardian of the soul…bringing you to new heights of awareness with her craft and passionate flair. She is a rock, with soft edges and authentic vulnerabilities. Do not mistake her kindness for ignorance..she is SPIRIT and can see truth. She has shed her many veils. She was born with the power to see through your exterior to your soul.

She exudes a balance of strength, vulnerability, openness and drive. She is a mover and a shaker and she will shake your ego until you let your soul out to be heard. Her courage isn't to be feared though, as her heart holds the world in its own hands. Her heart is a magnet, drawing those to her who seek more in life than the mundane.

BIG HAIR of loveliness, she comes alive when you bear witness to your own power and strength—as she is nothing more than a guide and a life long change queen. She will take you on a journey to your Self many times over and you will never look back as you shed your own ego.

Her secret? EQUANIMITY, TRUST, INTUITION and UNCONDITIONAL LOVE. She offers these gifts to you through this book, YOGISYNERGY, YOGIS4YOGA, her classes, workshops and her accredited yoga teacher training/spiritual development program. Come and play with this spiritual warrior…your life will shift immediately.

Resources

Attwood, Janet and Chris. The Passion Test. New York: Penguin Group, 2006.

Beckwith, Michael Bernard. Spiritual Liberation. New York: ATRIA Books, 2008.

Judith, Anodea. Chakra Balancing Kit. Boulder: Sounds True, 2003.

Lasater, Judith. Living Your Yoga. Berkeley: Rodmell Press, 2000.

Myss, Caroline. Anatomy of the Spirit. New York: Random House, 1996.

Defy Gravity. Carlsbad, CA: Hay House, Inc., 2009.

Satchinada, Swami. The Complete Bhagavad Gita. Buckingham: Integral Yoga Publications, 1988.

The Living Gita. Buckingham: Integral Yoga Publications, 1988.

Yoga Sutras by Patanjali. Buckingham: Integral Yoga Publications, 1978.

Shimhoff, Marci. Happy for No Reason. New York: Free Press, 2008.

Tolle, Eckhart. A New Earth. New York: Penguin Group, 2005.

The Power of Now. Vancouver, BC: Namaste Publishing, 1999.

Walsch, Neale Donald. Conversations with God. New York: Hampton Roads Publishing, 1995.

Happier Than God. Ashland: Emnin Books, 2008.